Clothing Optional

To my two cousins with lots & lots of love forever!

Jules
XXoo

Clothing Optional

◆

Sassy Essays from My First 50 Years

Julietta Appleton

Writer's Showcase
New York Lincoln Shanghai

Clothing Optional
Sassy Essays from My First 50 Years

All Rights Reserved © 2001, 2003 by Julietta Appleton

No part of this book may be reproduced or transmitted in any form or by any means, graphic, electronic, or mechanical, including photocopying, recording, taping, or by any information storage retrieval system, without the written permission of the publisher.

Writer's Showcase
an imprint of iUniverse, Inc.

For information address:
iUniverse, Inc.
2021 Pine Lake Road, Suite 100
Lincoln, NE 68512
www.iuniverse.com

ISBN: 0-595-26528-6

Printed in the United States of America

Almost all of the following essays first appeared either in the Lewisboro Ledger or the Bedford Record Review (newspapers in Westchester County, NY—1 hour north of that teeming, sinning, über-chic metropolis, The Big Apple,) between 1996 and 2002. If a real named is used, it is with the individual's permission. Otherwise, names have been changed to protect the privacy of those who would be crazy to let me write about them.

J.A.

Contents

Happy Unbirthday to Me................................ 1
In the Good Ole Valentimes............................ 4
The Perils of Penguinas............................... 6
Grunions and Husbands................................ 10
A Daughter Goes to College........................... 12
Giving up the Bird................................... 15
Never a Dull Woman................................... 18
Waking the Dead at Forest Lawn....................... 21
Adult Language....................................... 25
This Ain't No Knee-Jerk, Baby!....................... 28
Baby Animals... 31
The Search for a Good Cuppa.......................... 34
Heavy Objects.. 37
Too Hot to Handle.................................... 40
Alice in Dildoland................................... 42
Roos, Vhy Vass I in da Hospital?..................... 46
So, Was It Good for Me?.............................. 49
Halfway to Alte Kokkerdom............................ 53
Lost and Found....................................... 56

Floyd Joy, Floyd Joy, Floyd Joy 58
Phobobabes 62
Rage Against the Machine 65
Hair Today, Gone Tomorrow 67
Common Discourtesy 69
Road Warriors 74
The Electronic Version of Crack 76
The Summer of Our Discontent 79
Decorating with "Wrong Shui" 83
This Dog's Life 86
Health and Beauty Tips from Gals on the Go 89
I'll Have the Cyanide, Hold the Mayo 91
Unorthodox Exes 94
Meet and Delete 97
Cronehood's Only Just Begun 99
Clothing Optional 102
Godiva's Got Nothing on Me 105
Big Boy Cars 108
Press This! 110
You Do the Math 112
Singin' in the Pain 115
Salon Secrets Revealed! 118
Libby Gets a Nose Job 120
Puttin' on the Kitsch 123

How I Found Peace in the Information Age 125
Star-Crossed Driver. 127
Yes, I Have no Bananas. 130
Mailbox Macho 132
The Big Five-Oh. 134

Acknowledgments

For Treacy, who thought this would be a good idea; for John, who said reading this was like dating me for six months and who will live in my heart always; for Aunt Mary, who made this book possible; for my Pussy Posse (you know who you are) who put the quality in my quality of life; and for Noah and Miriam, my blessings and pillars of strength.

Happy Unbirthday to Me

Yesterday would have been my birthday, if it had been February 29th instead of March 1st. Whenever people ask me when my birthday is, and I say leap year (or more correctly, leap day), the inevitable response is, "It figures."

I'm still trying to figure out why it figures. And whose fault is it anyway? My mother's, for planning an elective Caesarean so I would be born before her doctor's vacation, not after, or Julius Caesar's, who invented leap year day in the first place?

Leap year is a contrivance so that the Julian calendar (named for good ole Julius, above) doesn't get too far away from the solar year. The time it takes the earth to go around the sun is not 365 days, it's 365 ¼ days, so every four years we add an extra day, my birthday, February 29th, so that 200 years from now Christmas doesn't come in autumn.

Here's the way it works: Every year divisible by 4 is a leap year, EXCEPT the last year of each century (like 1900, which was not a leap year), EXCEPT when the number of the century is a multiple of 4 (like 2000, which was a leap year), EXCEPT the year 4,000 and its later multiples (like 8,000 and 12,000, which won't be leap years). That's clear, right? If it is, you're way ahead of me on this.

Only 1 person in 1,461 is born on a leap day. That's just 0.0684% of the population, 200,000 of us in the United States, 4 million worldwide. I've met other leapers (or leapies, or leap dayers), as we're called. I went to a weensy Waldorf school in California with another one, Michael S., and for our "first" birthday (we were 4, in case the math is eluding you) a reporter and photographer came from the local newspaper and made me kiss Michael in front of a cake with one candle on it.

We were both embarrassed, but we sure looked cute. I wish I had a copy of that photo today.

In high school, I met another leaper. And a woman at the local DMV always remembers me because her nephew and I share the same unusual birthday. There are even clubs for us, such as the Honor Society of Leap Day Babies (www.leapdaybabies.com), of which I am a member. Last year, I got Happy Birthday emails from fellow leapers all over the world.

We leapers hear the same stuff over and over: "So, you're not really [insert age here]! You're [divide it by 4]! Forever young!" Yeah, well one look at me, and you know I'm not 11, okay? I'm sick of getting coloring books and dollies for my birthdays, and other leapers are just as exasperated by their juvenile gifts.

Another question we always get is, "When do you celebrate your birthday?" On February 29th, of course. In non-leap years, some of us are strict Februarians, so if there's no 29th, there's no birthday. Others believe that since February 29th is always the 60th day of the year, we leapers should celebrate on March 1st, the 60th day of the year in non-leap years. But many leapers, like me, celebrate on two days, February 28th and March 1st.

One non-leap year I decided to make another date my birthday. It was September 19th and I was sitting in a restaurant that offered free dinners on birthdays. So I presented my driver's license to the waitress, who showed it to the manager, who felt bad for me and gave me a free meal. All right, I admit, it was just a cheesy diner, but still, it was a thrill to get something in a birthday-deprived year.

I've also heard of leapers who really play the pity card and celebrate all week in non-leap years. This drives their families crazy. But I think it makes up for the leap years, particularly last year, which was/wasn't the millennium and was also one hell of a leap year. If you're a leaper, no one forgets your birthday when leap year rolls around. It can be overwhelming.

I can only speak for myself, but I'm willing to bet every leaper experienced what I did in the year 2000. The first phone call came at 7 AM-my college roommate, who rises at 5 to meditate and wanted to be my first leap day greeter. She was, with a sweet soprano rendition of Las Mañanitas, the traditional Mexican birthday song. The phone did not stop ringing all day, nor did the bell outside my front door stop gonging.

The package and flower deliveries continued all day. By late afternoon my house looked like a funeral parlor and I hadn't had time to shower, get dressed or eat. Well, I did eat one of my Krispy Kreme donuts, delivered by FedEx "fresh" from Chicago. The day was exhausting. I was glad when midnight arrived, and the calls finally stopped.

I'm not complaining exactly. It's pretty neat to be a leaper. But a lot of people think we're peculiar, abnormal, eccentric even. I hope that's not what anyone means when they tell me "it figures" that I have a leap day birthday. I prefer to think that I, and my fellow leapers, are simply special. Special in the best sense of the word.

In the Good Ole Valentimes

A long, long time ago, I used to look forward to Valentine's Day with great anticipation.

I used to start noodging my mother about a week before the Big Day to buy little red cards, red hots, candy hearts that said stuff like "Be mine" and "Sweet Heart," and doilies so I could make my own cards with red construction paper. My mother, who shopped at the health food store in the 1950's and forced us to eat only organic produce, was not thrilled at the idea of sugar coming into her house. But she let me eat it because it was a special occasion. Her disapproval only heightened my thrill.

To be honest, I can't say I even knew what the holiday, if it is indeed even a "holy" day, was all about. In my little-girl mind, it was a jumble consisting of cards, candy, Cupid, and, for some strange reason (maybe because it sounded like it?), Richie Valens. I couldn't even pronounce it right. My whole kindergarten class called it Valentimes Day, with an "m."

All I knew was that starting the first week of February, my little heart began to pound with excitement under my starched dresses because on Valentimes Day I was going to score. I'd go to school with cards and sweets and sticky artwork smelling of white paste for every kid in my class, and especially for my teacher. And I'd come home from school with a fat envelope with my name on it and lots of cards and candy.

Did I know from romance, or love, or anything that would make me blush at the thought of giving a boy a card that swore undying love? Or that scoring would have a completely different meaning when I got older? No way! This was straightforward, a strictly trading-post kind of exchange. There was none of the angst, say, of a first kiss. Everyone was happy. Except for my kindergarten Valentimes Day, when I got into trouble with Timmy Scharff.

I'm not sure who got into more trouble, me for being the perp or him for letting me be one. But I do know that in those days of approved spanking, both Timmy and I got our butts reddened but good. All because I got carried away with the scissors when we were cutting out red paper in class.

I guess I must have liked him just a little bit, because I paid a lot of attention to him. I think I even went home really happy that day, pleased at how I'd cut his bangs. I thought his freckled little face looked so cute now that I could see more of it. But his mother didn't think so. And when the phone rang and it was her on the line, the red hots stopped tasting so good on my tongue.

Today, Valentine's Day doesn't mean very much to me except an excuse to buy myself red hots. It's still a jumble, with added features that include the St. Valentine's Day Massacre, NECCO (New England Confectionery Company, out of Cambridge, MA, who make the weensy hearts with sayings), diamond engagement rings (not that I ever got one), heart-shaped tubs in the Poconos (nix on that too, thank goodness) and of course, Timmy Scharff. My first kiss? Well, it wasn't on Valentine's Day and it wasn't in kindergarten and it wasn't with Timmy. But Timmy, if you ever read this, I'm blowing you a kiss and wishing you a Happy Valentimes. And I'm sorry about your hair.

The Perils of Penguinas

Often I find myself with friends who begin to discuss their educational experiences in Catholic schools. They talk about how strict the nuns were (the teachers were usually nuns, with the exception of some male friends who were taught by Jesuit priests). They talk about how freely the nuns smacked, whacked, swatted and paddled for infractions ranging from gum chewing to talking aloud in class.

My friends are always astonished when I say, "Oh, I remember all that so well!" Eyebrows raise, then knit together quizzically.

"But you're Jewish," they finally muster, as if this is something I don't know. Yes, I am Jewish, but I attended various Catholic boarding and day schools during the three years I spent in Europe as a teenager.

Picture me, a skinny, curly-haired girl, sassy and terrified at the same time, living at Santa Dorotea, a Catholic boarding school in northern Italy. The dormitory consisted of rows and rows of beds, just like in the children's book *Madeline*; perhaps twenty beds in each of the five rows. Each bed had a little dresser next to it. The floors were marble, the ceilings were twenty feet high. The wooden blinds were closed against the heat so the room was dark with rectangular lines of light bordering each ten-foot tall window.

There were crucifixes everywhere, on walls, hanging from the necks of the students and the wimpled sisters, hanging from beaded wooden belts on the nuns' black habits. Statues of Mary and Jesus were all around, some of them dripping life-like looking blood.

All the little girls were Italian, except me. All of them had rosaries, except me. All of them had a clue what the symbols and rituals meant, except me.

The Perils of Penguinas 7

The first evening that the bells rang for vespers, I lay on my bed reading while everyone queued up. Realizing the severity of my ignorance, one of the girls grabbed me by the hand and pulled me into line. We all silently walked on the crunchy gravel to the chapel, where we all dipped our fingers in a big stone bowl of water, genuflected and sat down. I was shoved into a pew, given whispered instructions in Italian (which I didn't understand), and was guarded closely.

I figured the best way to learn the local customs was to observe and copy my dorm mates. To paraphrase, "when in Italy, do as the Italians do." I stood when they stood, knelt when they knelt, sat when they sat, crossed myself when they did. Then came the parade to the altar, or so I thought.

We marched in a long line, then everyone knelt. Like baby birds, they opened their mouths, I opened my mouth. Then all hell broke loose.

The Mother Superior swooped down on me like a big black condor and pulled me off the frontlines. She was shouting, "No, no, no!" and some other stuff that included Italian words sounding like Jewish and First Communion in her tirade. She guided me firmly by my upper arm and pushed me down onto the seat of a pew.

My open-mouthed pals were aghast. The ones who'd taken communion had their mouths glued shut, but the surprise registered in their faces. My behavior was apparently sacrilegious and inappropriate. I should know from this? How, exactly, did anyone figure I'd know about all this?

From then on, I was banned from Holy Communion, but not from mass. Everyone else went to the altar, and Jew Girl sat alone, eyed suspiciously by the nuns.

These same nuns who were sticklers for appropriateness allowed us to purchase beer with lunch (we were 11 years old) and afterward buy unlimited amounts of candy from the school store, as long as we didn't throw the wrappers on the floors or grounds.

And of course, there was the whacking. Usually for a wrong answer, or for an impertinent question, or for talking back to a sister. No one was spared.

I'm sure you won't find it hard to believe that as far as impertinence went, I was excelling. After my public humiliation at the altar and subsequent scrutiny by classmates, who actually felt my head for horns and asked did I drink baby's blood, I was positively hissy. Growing up in Los Angeles I may have gotten the occasional *potch in tuchus* (Yiddish for swat on the butt) when I misbehaved around my parents or grandparents, but this regular abuse was downright extreme. And I didn't like it.

My career as a Catholic schoolgirl came to an end one sunny day, with the fruity scent of English boxwoods in the air, when Sister Carmela and I had a confrontation. We were outside, walking on the gravel path between buildings, discussing politics (remember, I'm 11). She asked me did I not think that President Kennedy was the best president the Americans ever had. In my rudimentary Italian I replied, "How should I know? I haven't been around long enough to know them all."

Smack. She landed a stinger across my cheek. I was furious. I looked her in the eye and shouted, "You…you…you PENGUINA!" I hoped it meant penguin in Italian.

Her jaw dropped, and in that small moment I ran back to the dormitory and began packing. I lugged my valise to the Mother Superior's office, walked straight to the phone without permission, and called my father.

"Get over here right away and get me out of here," I yelled, my tears flowing freely. "I don't belong here! I'm Jewish! I'm walking out the door now and you better come pick me up!"

No one stopped me. We all (except my father) knew I didn't belong there. I'm sure I deserved a *potch in tuchus* for being such a smart aleck, but if anyone was going to give it to me it was gonna be my Daddy.

I trudged down the dusty, lion-colored road, cypress trees on either side of me, dragging my suitcase. I wondered if my father would really come.

He did. After what seemed like forever, he pulled up across from me, got out of the car and put his arms around me.

"So," he asked, "you've had it with the *penguinas*, huh?"

Grunions and Husbands

I have finally figured out some important stuff about men. It can be narrowed down to two things: They have penises, and when you marry them (men, not penises, although sometimes they're interchangeable) they all become the same person. This insight is based not just on my personal experience, but also on the experiences of several married or divorced women friends.

We all agree. When men are courting, they are like grunions, those little California fish that passionately mate under the full moon during the three summer months. Men, like grunions, thrash and heave themselves at the women of their choice, eager to assert their biological imperative to reproduce. For men, this behavior includes actual talking, romance, alertness and sometimes eschewing athletic activities other than sexual congress. When men marry and get to sprinkle their magic silver seeds on a regular basis, their powers of speech atrophy, they are happy to eat cereal for dinner, and they take up snoring as a pastime, usually while "watching" anything on TV so long as it's got other men and some kind of ball (this is called "just resting their eyes").

The penis thing is of course what gets them, and us, into trouble. Men are driven by their genitalia. Even my highly esteemed, very professional girlfriend, Angela, calls men "the penis people", as if they were a species from a galaxy far, far away. An old Yiddish proverb maintains, "when the penis stands, the brains lie on the ground." Yet if we didn't like them (penises, not men), we'd marry other women.

Women don't usually ask, "What do you want me to say?" Or, "Where's the butter?" Or, "Have you seen the remote control?" Women tend to be communicative and resourceful and self-sufficient. Most of us don't snore, or subscribe to the Sports channel on cable.

But we don't have penises, and for most women I know, a penis is something we want in a man.

So we search for our soulmate, a man who is "compatible," whose list of attributes complements ours. We meet him in a bar, through a friend, a personal ad, by chance, online even. And in millions of bedrooms and hotel rooms around the world, the same thing happens. Boy meets girl, girl meets penis, boy falls asleep.

And we get married anyway. We sleep in each other's arms at night, make babies, pay the bills, go to soccer practice, and if we're lucky, grow old together. But our husbands never act like grunions again, never throw themselves at us with their linguistic and romantic charms exposed. (If your husband is still doing this, I say wait. You haven't been married long enough.)

Of course, all of this is gross generalization. But except for small modifications (one likes his meat and potatoes instead of Froot Loops, another prefers golf to basketball, another actually reads and writes poetry), men as husbands are pretty much interchangeable. Which isn't such a bad thing, because if you ever start thinking that the man you married isn't right for you and there is someone out there, unmet as yet, who would make a better husband, it's a comfort to know you're wrong.

Because once he finds you and woos you and drives you crazy and takes you to his bed, he will fall asleep. And he'll snore.

A Daughter Goes to College

In 1998 my husband and I took our second kid to college. It was rough. We returned home from the University of Pennsylvania in Philadelphia after spending almost a whole day shlepping FOUR golf-cart loads of our daughter Miriam's stuff up four flights to a sweltering single dorm room and getting her settled in. This move-in was very different from our son Noah's two years before that, which took tops two hours. For one thing, it didn't take us two months to adjust.

I hate to say it, because I consider myself a feminist, but girls really are different from boys. Noah moved with his stereo, guitar, conga, computer, one bag of clothes, his linens, and the laundry detergent and toiletries I had to remind him to bring. He kinda packed as he went out the door. No planning ahead for our boy. Too much of a commitment. To this day, he is not a planner. Which drives his girlfriend and us crazy. But we love him because he is brilliant, hysterically funny, a talented musician and a great cook.

Miriam on the other hand—the child who fed her Barbie dolls to the dogs and did head switching experiments on their remains; the child who Noah said was really the son my husband Bill never had—brought electronics and appliances of almost every imaginable kind (including a curling, or in her case uncurling, iron, microwave, stereo, TV, assorted lamps, and of course her superfast computer with zip drive), six bags of clothes for every occasion possible, so many shoes we called her Imelda as she packed, pillows, bed-rest (known, I kid you not, as a "husband"), down body pillow, several types of blankets and quilts, and more boxes of toiletries and makeup than Tammy Faye Baker could shake a lipstick at. (Miriam hardly ever wears anything more than lip-gloss.) Did I mention the full-length mirror, shelving (that Bill put together with much cursing, after he connected the computer), glow in the dark stars, plastic plates and silverware, foodstuffs and beer mugs? And my daughter, the intellectual, snobby, anti-Jewish-Princess jock had her NAILS painted for this auspicious occasion. In a color called "Wicked."

I know I had more trouble with this separation than I did with Noah's. Once again, my feminist sensibility rears its head and asks how could I love one child (the girl) more than another (the boy)? Of course I don't! That's not it at all. It's just that Noah seemed to handle his move to college in Boston with great ease and confidence. No tears beforehand (and he is a weeper), not nearly as many screaming fights with us as we had with Miriam. In fact, our fights with him were of a different variety, the slammed door and silence kind. Followed by apologies. On his moving-in day, students with huge laundry carts showed up at our car, and we were whisked up in an elevator to the 12th floor of his dorm. As soon as I had made up his bed, he announced, "Okay guys, I can handle it from here. Thanks a lot for helping me move." Hugs, kisses and we were gone. In the car, we cried (Bill is a weeper too). We cried at home. We cried on and off for about a month, and we recognized the same sad look in the faces of other parents we knew who'd also sent their sons off to college. Until the kids all returned home for a holiday weekend, it felt like there'd been a mass death in the family of our community.

Miriam started planning her college move in May, a month before she graduated from high school. There were lists everywhere, lists that changed almost daily (they got bigger, not smaller, as you may have guessed). Lists that were constant reminders that she was leaving us. Most of her shopping was done by June. To her credit, she paid for most of her new college belongings herself with money she earned from working. We paid for the basics, but we were not enablers in her addiction to shoes, make-up and expensive name-brand clothes. And lest you think Miriam is shallow and materialistic, let me *kvell* here (that's Yiddish for bursting with pride) and tell you that she graduated fourth in her class with seventeen awards for academic excellence and a scholarship package to her Ivy League school. She is majoring in medical bioethics and wants to save the world from the scourge of AIDS. Sometimes I can't believe this remarkable young woman is my kid.

So on Miriam's moving day into hallowed halls, what did I do? I guarded the bags and boxes and one teddy bear, Albeart Einstein, that didn't fit in the golf cart and had to be left on the street. I hid behind my sunglasses while people passed me and pointed, and laughed. Laughed. I arranged her furniture, and rearranged it, and rearranged it again. I swept her floor, dusted her furniture, hung her clothes. And I got criticized by Miriam for saying "Hi" back to all the people who passed her open door. "Do you HAVE to be so friendly?!!" she snapped. She wanted us gone, it was obvious, but she couldn't let us leave.

I convinced Bill, whose face was dripping sweat and had turned the color of his burgundy shirt, to take a dinner break with me. We promised Miriam we'd return to her room to say goodbye. Dinner was fun, relaxing, and best of all, the restaurant was air-conditioned. No one yelled at us—not that you'd expect that from a server, but back home in New York, that might have been a possibility—and we looked lots happier than the other moms and dads we saw around us, sitting with their terrified freshmen. Maybe, we wondered, it was actually going to be easier this time around? We returned to Miriam's room in the Quad, and she was showered, heading off to a house meeting and ready to say goodbye. She'd survived the two hours in her dorm without us. Hugs, kisses, and Bill and I left.

It seems hard to believe that after all the angst, separation fears, tears, fights followed by cuddles that went on for weeks, no, months, prior to Miriam's leaving, not one tear was shed by either of us on the way home. We were too tired. Or maybe we were just stunned by the realization that in May, we would have to bring all the stuff back home. But then we started to miss her so much, we almost looked forward to it.

Giving up the Bird

Twenty years ago a friend of mine abruptly became a vegetarian when she really gave some thought to the slaughter of millions of turkeys each year for Thanksgiving tables across America. She hasn't eaten anything that walks, swims or flies since.

I had no such dilemma. I wear leather. I eat meat, but I prefer it to look like it's as far away from its original source as possible. Like, don't serve me a whole fish with its eyes looking at me.

But this Thanksgiving I'm feeling differently about what to eat. Over the years we've transformed our menu as more ethnicities came aboard—we added Italian appetizers, African-American style veggies and Greek baklava for dessert. This year my daughter's a practicing Jew-Bu who eats no meat, but does eat fish. Buddhists supposedly don't eat anything with a soul; what I want to know is how anyone knows that Brussels sprouts don't have souls?

I suppose my latest quirk is not rational, either. I don't want to eat turkey. It's because I'm in love, with a cockatiel named Chuck.

My love of birds began when I got my first pair of binoculars 20 years ago. I counted, I kept lists of birds like scarlet tanagers and rose-breasted grosbeaks, but I still ate turkey. Then we got a Quaker parrot named Betty. A bright green ball of feathers who learned to say, "Hello!" and "I love you." Apparently my children taught her some other things, too, when I wasn't around, so sometimes when I was alone with her I'd hear someone cursing me out in the foulest language, and it was little Betty.

But Quakers are not always so nice. They bite. Hard. There's a reason these birds are illegal in Connecticut. A couple of Quakers can chew down an entire forest of trees in one year. So when Betty started hanging off my upper lip and drawing blood, I didn't mind it so much that my son put her on the floor and began using her to play Bowling with Birdie. Usually she got out of the way of the tennis ball, but not always.

When the biting got to be too much, we gave her back to the breeder who have us a cockatiel. Much smaller beak, much better disposition. We named him Cosmo, and he was wonderful. He whistled "I love you," liltingly, would make kissing noises, and could belt out The Mexican Hat Dance, Yellow Bird, and Hava Nagila. He would walk down the hall hissing at the cats, who were terrified of him, climb up the dust ruffle, perch himself on my chest and whistle to me and snuggle.

But when I got divorced, I got rid of Cosmo. My friends tell me that I complained, "Cosmo is too damn cheerful." I needed to be miserable. So I found Cosmo a happy home.

I pretty much forgot about bird ownership, and kept on eating smoked turkey breast like it came from a store, not an animal. And then I met Chuck, who lives at the local hardware store. He came out of his cage and perched on my shoulder and started making kissing sounds. He fluffed up, a sure sign a bird likes you, and imitated me as I taught him to whistle The Mexican Hat Dance. Every time I'd go in the store, I'd borrow a stepladder and get Chuck out of his cage. We loved each other.

A few weeks ago, I went to see my birdie boy, and he was gone. Moved to Florida. I was heartbroken. I took it personally. But last week, I found out he's back. Florida depressed him, so Diana (his human mother) went and got him and brought him back on Amtrak.

I can't wait to go visit him and get my kisses. And I can't even think about eating turkey this year. The idea that it comes from an animal that can say, "I love you" and kiss me gives me just enough creeps to abstain.

So in addition to all the other food we're having, I'm serving honey-glazed ham. I'm okay with this, for now. But I just found out that pigs are really smart, and have the IQ of kindergartners. At least pigs don't say "I love you." That'd be too much for me to handle in one Thanksgiving.

Never a Dull Woman

"Oh my God!" exclaimed a friend when he visited my house. "You're almost as bad as Mike."

"Bad how?" I asked. "What'd I do?"

"Your house. It's so *clean*."

"And this is a problem why?" I asked.

"Well, when do you have time to do it?" he asked politely but suspiciously.

"I make time. Otherwise I can't find anything."

"I'm envious. On a neatness scale of a hundred, you're a 95. I'm a 75, on a good day."

"And Mike?"

"One twenty," he proclaimed about his best friend.

I laughed, but I admit I was embarrassed. Almost ashamed that I had a neat, orderly house, and troubled that I wanted to be like Mike. I wanted to be better than one twenty. I kept envisioning a doormat I'd once seen that said, "A clean house is the sign of a dull woman." Fears of obsessive-compulsive disorder gripped me.

Then I came to my normal, pissed-off senses. What the hell is so wrong with a clean house, anyway?

In my opinion, a dirty house is the sign of a disorganized mind. Female or male. Why do I feel the need to defend what makes tremendous sense to me and most of the world?

A certain amount of dirt and clutter is to be expected in the homes of people who really live there. I think we all have dust bunnies under our beds, and that's okay. A few dirty dishes soaking in the sink overnight, also okay. Unread newspaper, magazines and books piling up on the coffee table? Fine. If they're in an orderly pile…

But living in wall-to-wall chaos would drive me insane. I can sit on the couch at one dear, and brilliant, friend's house and invariably stand up with bits of hardware and spare change stuck to me. His house, on the Appleton scale, is a minus ten.

On the other extreme is a beloved girlfriend in California who used to label and alphabetize her spices. Maybe she still does. She's at the top of the scale, next to a neighbor of mine who owns four "spaghetti" mops ("I don't like the way any of them cleans," she says) and is still searching for the perfect one. And Mrs. Whitegloves' daughter in Montreal has come a long way. Although her sock drawer could pass military inspection, with socks rolled and ordered by color and weight, she can let her dishes *air* dry in the rack now.

In the middle, just like on any bell curve, are the folks who hate the mess but don't have the time to fix it, or to pay someone else to. And sometimes only you can remedy a mess, like organizing files. Asking someone else to do it leaves you perplexed, frustrated and lost. Out of control.

Control is probably what motivates most of us to clean or not to clean. Me, I've been uprooted and transplanted so many times I have the ability to make a house a home in record time. I feel relaxed when I know things are where I expect to find them (unlike some of the people in my life, who've gone and come, or gone and stayed gone). I can also relax when I'm sitting in someone else's mess, say, picking screws off my ass. That's because it's not my problem, not my space to control.

But when it's my environment, here are the rules:

No whiskers or pubes in the tub or sink. No pee on or around the toilet. No dirty dishes anywhere except the sink, and there's a time limit on how long they can stay there before they are hand-washed or put in the dishwasher. No sticky floors. No stinky garbage. No unmade beds. And above all, no ashtrays, empty or full, anywhere.

Am I mentally ill because I like a clean house? Because I fluff the pillows on my couch? Because I cannot imagine a life without a Dust-buster? I don't think so. There are people I love very much who did have cleaning compulsions, and they got help in the form of therapy or medications. I'll get help too if I find myself washing my hands until they're raw, or if I find myself arranging the Fiestaware in rainbow order again. I did it once, and I scared myself.

But daily bed making as a psychological flaw? Because someone thinks I'm bored and have nothing better to do? Get oudda here! I'm not buying it no matter how many doormats are selling it. I may be neat and clean. But dull? Never.

Waking the Dead at Forest Lawn

I recently visited friends and family in the land of la-la, where I am originally from. It's been 17 years since I was "home", and although many things have changed in Los Angeles, more have not. The sky is still smoggy, nearly everyone is still "in the business", orange trees are everywhere, they still have earthquakes, and Forest Lawn is still Forest Lawn.

When my mother died, I was only 9 years old, yet I was aware of the controversy in my family regarding her request to be buried in a non-denominational cemetery. My Orthodox Jewish grandparents were *plotzing* that their daughter was not only going to a non-kosher burial site, but that she had requested to be cremated, another Jewish no-no. They bribed my father $5,000 to have her buried at neighboring Mount Sinai cemetery, but he respected my mother's last wishes to be at Forest Lawn.

The last time I had been to my mother's grave was thirty years ago. I knew that during this visit to California it was my obligation to pay my respects, but I avoided it. Not that being dead is such a negative thing in L.A., since there's a real smorgasbord of choices that reflect one's pre-termination status in life. A friend tells me her family members have chosen a lovely black marble mausoleum in West L.A., one that holds a couple hundred chosen people. It's deluxe and boasts location, location, location. Her relatives will be right next to Jack Benny, in good company in the big beyond. And Marilyn's there too.

Cemeteries in L.A. do not have the panache of our historic plots here in the East. (I say "our" because it was repeatedly pointed out to me in L.A. that I am no longer a Californian, I talk too fast and have too much Noo Yawk attitude.) No faded tombstones, no hundreds of years of history, no quiet dignity. Death in Hollywood is still showbiz.

To gear up for my visit to Forest Lawn, I got a massage from a singer/actress/waitress/masseuse who was cutting her first CD of original songs, "sort of a country Sara McLachlan." I ate a lot of Mexican food, mostly from cheap dives whose authentic *chile rellenos* far surpassed any Mexican cuisine available in New York (except for Rosa Mexicano in New York City, which is not a dive, but charges trendy gourmet prices). I lay by the pool. I watched every video of films up for any kind of Oscar (my friend is "in the business" and is a voting member of the Academy). And then, on a rare day with clear blue skies, my friend Liane and I drove to Forest Lawn.

To get there, we took the crowded freeway past the old Buena Vista studios, now called Disney Studios. The entire facade has been redone in 1930's art deco style, and from a distance, the first thing you see is an enormous replica of Mickey Mouse's hat in the Sorcerer's Apprentice. The giant blue cone, covered with celestial shapes, pierces the sky and rises far above the studio. On the other side of the building, perched on the roof and each standing perhaps 20 feet high, are Snow White's seven colorful dwarves. It's rumored that the designer had a fight with Disney Studios and constructed the dwarves so that when it rains, it looks like they're peeing on the studio. Revenge, Hollywood style.

We entered Forest Lawn through the security booth in front of the chapel, by a sign that advertises loudly, "One call or visit: Undertaking, cemetery, church and flowers." It reminded me of the way I used to facetiously answer the phone in high school, by saying, "Raskin's morgue—you kill 'em, we chill 'em." I'm wondering what my mother, who was new-age forty years before her time, saw in this almost garish place. I mean, this woman was into homeopathic medicine, chiropractic care, coffee enemas, health food, organic eggs, homemade bread, freshly extracted juices for breakfast, and the occasional psychic reading. Forest Lawn just did not seem her style. For her ending I would have imagined a tender sprinkling of ashes in the Muir Woods, perhaps, not a place that advertises on a billboard. But I'm sure she had her reasons.

I got directions from the booth to my mother's gravesite—Hillside, Space 4, Lot 5547. As we drove past all kinds of statues, including an enormous one of Moses on a throne, we heard music wafting our way. A short distance down the hill was a 25-piece Mariachi band playing a lively *jarabe* for a funeral. It was beautiful.

We parked at the curb of Hillside and started our search. Spaced among the flat bronze plaques embedded in the grass are circular cement markers with numbers. Addresses of the deceased. They were impossible to figure out, especially if you are in an emotional state, which I imagine anyone visiting a grave is bound to be.

Liane and I split up, wandering barefoot in the lush grass of Hillside like deranged ants on a mission. Periodically we'd shout out numbers to each other, "Five five four three!" or "Five seven two one! I think I've gone too far!" Finally, "Five five four seven!" But we still were not in the right place. Up, down, back up, back down, calling out the names on the plaques like drill sergeants.

"Mommeeeeeeeeee!" I yelled in exasperation, "Where ARE you?"

I sat down on the grass, frustrated. Next to me was the plaque of a dentist who'd died in 1988. I began to laugh out loud. His epitaph read, "I told you I was sick."

Liane came over, read the plaque, and began to laugh too. My laughter increased to near hysteric proportion, the kind of mirth you experience in third grade when your best friend has just said a funny and you know you'll get in trouble if the teacher catches you laughing. You try to keep it to yourself, because of the circumstances, but the laughter explodes out of your nose and mouth in volcanic eruptions.

There I was at Forest Lawn cemetery, guffawing, tears streaming down my face. Across the freeway I could see the wizard's cap and some of the dwarves, and I laughed harder. I felt like I should be sent to the office to stand in the corner until I could behave myself.

Finally, wiping my eyes, we walked back to the car to start our hunt all over. And not four feet from us, in the first row, was my mother's grave. Betty Raskin Appleton, March 24, 1911—June 18, 1961. Her epitaph reads, "She gave so much to so many."

Yes she did. Not the least of which is my ability to see the humor in even the saddest moments, which is a priceless legacy. Thank you Mommy.

Adult Language

Right after I had kids, I became a childbirth educator. It was a great way to get paid for nursing in front of an audience and calling it hands-on teaching. I taught about labor and birth and postpartum until my kids were so postpartum they were applying to colleges and could no longer be used as props. And I thought, after teaching almost 200 couples, that I had seen it all. But I hadn't really, until I taught my last series of classes.

The first night of class I set the pillows in a circle on the floor of my basement, anxious to meet my six new couples. Introductions went smoothly; this was going to be a cohesive, fun group. I had no idea how much fun. When Karen and Paul (not their real names) introduced themselves, Paul told us that both he and his wife had Tourette's syndrome. Karen was a blinker, but Paul shouted obscenities. He apologized in advance for offending anyone. I looked around the room, and though everyone seemed surprised, they appeared accepting.

One father-to-be asked, "What do we do? How should we react?"

"Go ahead and laugh," Karen said. "He's usually very funny. But if it gets annoying, just tell us 'tic break' and we'll go out for a walk or something."

And so I proceeded to outline the course content for the next ten weeks. I explained that we'd cover breastfeeding and new parenthood, too, not just labor and birth.

"Most parents come home with their baby and wonder 'Now what do we do?'" I said.

"Feed the little fuck! Feed the little fuck! Feed the little fuck!" Paul shouted as he wrenched his head rapidly toward his left shoulder.

First, there was stunned silence. I mean a long stunned silence. And then, raucous howling laughter, the tears-streaming-down-our-faces kind.

"That's exactly right Paul!" I said, after I regained some composure. "You're gonna make a great dad."

Somehow I got through that first class and the next nine. With Paul there, it was like having a heckler. When I discussed how drugs could cause birth defects in the first trimester, and used Thalidomide as an example, Paul shouted "Flippers! Flippers!" to our great mortification. In discussing the difference in training between doctors and midwives, all I got out of my mouth was "Doctors…" before Paul yelled "…suck! Doctors suck!" "Get to the point, bitch!" he would often yell at me if I wasn't moving the class fast enough. The thirteen of us spent a lot of time in helpless heaps on the floor, laughing until we ached.

Forget trying to show videos. They made Paul really crazy. We discovered this one night when we watched a film showing several births. Every time Paul saw naked women giving birth, he'd yell obscenities about female genitalia. He punctuated the film with meows, for emphasis. We were constantly stopping the videos for tic breaks.

"I dunno about you guys," said Karen finally, "but I think Paul is too distracting. We'll go home now and borrow the video before the next class. Okay with you?"

"Sure," said another soon-to-be-dad. He got up and put his arms around Paul. "Ya gotta chill out, bro!"

"Meow," Paul meekly replied.

I wasn't sure anyone had learned anything in that class series. But I was wrong.

Paul and Karen and the other five couples came back for a reunion after all six babies were born. We ate and drank and laughed. Everyone shared their birth stories and showed off their newborns.

"Hey Paul, how did the nurses handle you at the birth? Were you treated well?" asked one new daddy, protectively.

"Oh, they were great. I think I shocked them, but it was nothing compared to how I cursed the rabbi out at our wedding. We have it on video."

"The birth?"

"Both. Wedding and birth."

"I'd pay to see that!"

"You don't have to. Come over, we'll show it to you."

Although I don't teach anymore, this groups still meets. Once a year they have a reunion with their toddlers, and now there are even some baby brothers and sisters. Sometimes I go, but the circle has really closed around them, and I'm glad. Karen told me that before my class, Paul hadn't been out of the house to anything social in over five years. Now they have new friends.

Even though both of their children have the Tourette's gene, they may not develop Tourette's syndrome. And they might just have tics, or be blinkers, not cursers. But, even if they do become cursers and are half as brilliant and entertaining as their daddy, that would be okay too.

This Ain't No Knee-Jerk, Baby!

If you haven't dated recently, then you're lucky. I say this because I have, and I'm starting to understand expressions like, "I'd enjoy root canal more," or, "I'd rather gargle with glass."

Imagine sitting in a lovely restaurant, across the table from the hunk of your dreams, as he tells you that he thinks all gay people choose to be abnormal and all black people are murderers. Picture the food dribbling down your chin as you gawk in amazement at the Jurassic mentality of this used-to-look-good-from-afar individual.

When I recount this true adventure, no one is surprised. Such attitudes, I'm told, are prevalent. Everyone has their "quirks." QUIRKS? Say what??? Where have I been?

Look, I admit it. I'm a child of the sixties. Make love not war, to the max! Woe unto him who disparaged another's race, creed, or sexual orientation, although we women *did* brew the coffee for our brother revolutionaries, and allowed ourselves to be called "chicks." Then we got pissed off, burned our bras and assumed our rightful places. Sorta. I was raised on the pap of correctness, political or otherwise. But it was never knee-jerk, which implies reflexive, behavior.

The "L" word has come to be almost as bad as the "N" word. But liberalism is not always an instinctive reaction, it is more often a well thought-out stance that many of us choose to assume. We do so mindfully because we believe strongly in things like doing unto others as you would have them do unto you, and that all men (and women) are created equal. All that corny, biblical and patriotic stuff that the Christian right has thrown into our left-of-center faces as if they invented it. But we flower children have tried to live it.

Or so I thought. Maybe my generation was all about t-t-talk. Jerry Rubin runs networking parties, Grace Slick is in AA, and Bob Dylan is unintelligible. Jimi and Janis are long gone, joined recently by Timothy Leary (what did he do but coin an expression?) and Allen Ginsburg. The authors of the NIMBY (Not in My Backyard) philosophy are baby boomers, selfish yuppies who resist social welfare programs if they're too close to home. And one of the coolest people in the year 2000 was the man whose money you wanted to win, Ben Stein, and he has always been a conservative Republican. Oy, it's enough to give me *agida*. Pass the Prevacid, please, as I watch my dreams evaporate.

Trying to meet a likeminded man in my age group is a real challenge. Of course I've heard "all the good ones are taken," but I don't believe that because I'm one of the good ones. Or maybe that expression means all the good *men* are taken. Ya think? I don't really know, as I never dated before. That's another thing my generation didn't really do. No appointment was necessary for free love. We just got it on. So learning the rituals of courting is a brand-new experience.

I do know enough to know when someone's a jerk, and that a second date is just not going to happen. But how do you rule out the jerks before you even go out on that first date? How do you decide that even becoming "just friends" is as remote as successfully landing a spacecraft on Mars? How do you politely say, "I wish you'd fall into a black hole and leave me the fuck alone forever and ever, amen?"

My friend's husband asks me what did I expect from men anyway? He cites Chris Rock's assertion that men never have women friends, only women they haven't fucked yet. If this is true, and I am starting to fear that it is, then I may as well be in a relationship with a woman. Abnormal as that may be to some people with prehistoric mentalities.

I look at it this way. What I want in my life now is someone to snuggle up with every night, cook with, share walks in the woods and on the beach with, someone to watch the Knicks and *Win Ben Stein's Money* with, someone who will bring me soup if I'm sick. Did I mention sex? No. An electric appliance does the trick just fine, and doesn't leave a wet spot in the bed. It's the human connection I crave, and since women are my best friends anyway, why not?

Perhaps this logic would fuel Mr. Jurassic's argument that we abnormal folk choose to be that way. Damn straight I do, if he's behind Door B. His generalities make me burn with rage. My mommy and daddy taught me to respect everyone, not everyone except moolies or spics or dykes or Republicans or even racist, homophobic Jews. But I wouldn't want my daughter, or son, marrying one. And I certainly don't have to either.

Baby Animals

It's spring, finally. I can tell because little green shoots are popping up like crazy, my magnolias and dogwoods and crabapples are in bloom, and there's baby animals everywhere. Not yet the kind that nature produces, but the kind you are urged to buy right around Easter time. Bunnies, chicks, goslings. Things that are cute but poop a lot.

I know a lot about baby animals because somehow or other, I used to get my parents to succumb to my spring yearning—and it was a yearning—to possess a feathered friend or two. I remember Gracie, my goose, and Donald and Daisy, my ducks, and Chirpy, my Bantam hen who laid eggs in my lap, and the three white leghorns that Chirpy raised from fertilized eggs put in her nest (my brilliant idea). It was a howl to see this tiny ginger-colored chicken bossing around three children who were the chicken equivalents of Shaquille, Kareem and His Airness.

And what I also remember is the poop. Amazing quantities of it in my kiddie pool (Donald and Daisy needed a swimming hole) and around the garden and even in the house, because I convinced my parents that since I didn't have a dog like normal children did, my chickens should be allowed in the house. What I have chosen to forget is how my pets were disappeared at the kosher butcher, thanks to my grandmother, and that perhaps I even, without knowing, ate them.

This year I heard that a friend of mine succumbed, and got baby guinea hens (to protect his family against Lyme disease, of course!) and baby goats. Or kids, they're called—simply smaller versions of garbage-eating poop machines that will grow up to eat more garbage and leave bigger piles of goat poop. I think he fancies himself a gentleman farmer and boutique cheese producer. I think he's crazy.

I admit that the fondest memories of my childhood are of the times my father and I saved baby birds. In California we had lots of fruit trees, and every year at least one baby would fall from its nest and we couldn't get it back up into the tree. So we kept them warm in boxes of shredded newsprint placed carefully atop the stove over the pilot light, fed them homemade gruel from an eye-dropper, and when they were ready, I was allowed the privilege of teaching them to fly.

I'd run sprints in our backyard with a wobbly bird clutching my finger for dear life, and eventually, to save herself, she'd spread her wings and figure out she could let go. After a few days of this, we'd see her go for good. And I'd cry.

Being a junior wildlife rescuer was probably the most valuable lesson my father ever taught me about how to love, nurture, and be willing to let go. It didn't happen overnight, of course. For years I'd have to imagine that little birds in the trees were twittering and pointing, "There she is! That's her! Isn't she wonderful? She saved me!" in order not to feel like I had abandoned my charges.

But I no longer succumb to the guiles of baby anything.

My moment of clarity came last week when I met a girlfriend for coffee at our local, chichi Eurocafé. She and I, both past presidents of Westchester-Putnam Childbirth Education Association, both labor doulas who have attended over 150 births between us, both lactation consultants, both mothers who had babies at home with midwives and who breastfed our children, looked at the stroller brigade and rolled our eyes.

"Let's get out of here," she said. "Too many babies. We won't be able to have a conversation. I used to think this was so cute. What's happened to me?"

"I dunno," I answered. "But it's happened to me too. As sweet as they are, I am glad they're someone else's. And I'm glad I can walk away."

Now I look at those cute Easter bundles, furred, feathered, whatever, and think what messes they make. Who needs that responsibility? Let someone else be a sucker and succumb.

I've done my time, made my personal and professional contribution to mothers, babies, and baby animals. I have cleaned up more poop than I care to recall. I still love to be present at births, snuggle and sniff newborns and infants, even baby-sit on occasion.

But, believe it or not, I actually like teenagers better. I should probably have my head examined. Maybe spring has gotten to me after all.

The Search for a Good Cuppa

Every day around 4PM, my friend's mother-in-law, a Londoner, used to quip, "I could murder a good cuppa!" Cuppa, of course, is cup of tea. I understand completely how she feels.

In the United States, our deep connection to tea apparently ended when those angry colonists sent it to the bottom of the Boston harbor, where I hear it is still polluting the water.

To this day, most Yanks wake up and need their cup of 'joe,' 'java,' or 'grande latte with soy milk' (arrrrrrrrgh-if I were a coffee bean, I'd go on strike from such an abuse). Coffee rules here. Without it, medical schools would collapse. Writers would be grouchy. The phone company would not show up on time. Oh wait, I mean they would not show up at all.

But there are those of us whose family histories include tea, and tea lore. For example, my godfather, Anton Chekhov's nephew, left Russia in the late 1940's to escape Stalin. During his journey to the United States, tea was plentiful but sugar was not. Like all Russians, he and his traveling companions drank their tea from glasses. If they preferred sweet tea, they held the sugar cube between their teeth.

At one of their hideouts, they sat down for tea, hung their last sugar cube from the light bulb string and spun it in a circle. As it swung past each man, he raised his glass and drank. Since they were all Stanislavsky Method actors, they could imagine its sweetness, or so I was told.

I learned to love tea from my Russian-born father. Milk and sugar, please. My tea must be strong enough to hold its flavor when the milk is added. My cuppa has to look just so, the exact color of a camel hair coat. Or else.

My favorite meal (and now my daughter's too) is what Americans call "high tea." In Britain it's a snack, a time to drop your burdens and relax. No jacket required. It's nothing too fancy unless you go to a shop. And it's just called 'tea,' although it's way more than a cuppa. First, finger sandwiches with cucumber and watercress and butter, curried shrimp salad, egg salad, smoked salmon with dill, and often more. Then scones with clotted or Devonshire cream (nothing else has a flavor like it) and jams, followed by tiny desserts (which I can never finish because I have eaten three times too many finger sandwiches). All accompanied by one's own pot of tea-lapsang souchong with its smoky perfume, oolong, orange pekoe, Formosa, Earl Grey, or one of the Breakfasts, English or Irish.

I make it my business to sample high tea wherever it's offered. I've had outrageously priced high tea in New York City at the former Helmsley Palace where Leona, rhymes-with-witch, made my ex put on a polyester brocade sport jacket to sit and sip. It was okay, if you like painted cherubs on the ceiling and a harpist plonking away during your meal. Because of the burgundy monstrosity the ex was forced to wear, the waitress looked down her nose at us. I was glad when my ex stuck his size 11 dirty sneakers out from under the damask tablecloth, and we giggled every time Miss-Holier-Than-Thou walked by and sniffed in disdain.

In Manhattan, Little Nell's used to be great, on York and 85th. Mismatched china, great prices, good strong tea. But it's gone. The Stanhope and St. Regis are nice, but pricey. Danal is nice, down on Astor place. The last time I was there, the waiter gasped when I said "Lapsang please," and said, "Oooh honey, now that is Harley Davidson tea!" The T Salon is also lovely, if pricey.

In our area, there's not much. I've had high tea locally at a very posh museum and the tea was as pale as wee wee. When I complained, and asked for a stronger pot, I was told, "This is how it's supposed to be." I wanted to scream, "I've been to Harrod's! Have you? This is NOT how it's s'posed to be!"

There are some other people who understand the importance of tea. My neighbors import their St. Michael's extra strong tea—one bag makes a whole pot—from Marks and Spencer. Then again, they're Canadians and still like to think they're British subjects. But I'm with them. Personally, I think world peace could begin with the perfect cuppa.

Heavy Objects

In a recent TV show, two detectives enter a lesbian bar and one of the cops is aghast and agape at all the beautiful women paired with each other. He hadn't expected "those" kind of women to be gay.

"Oh yeah," says his partner, "once they can lift heavy objects by themselves, we're obsolete."

It's not just lifting heavy objects that gives us women a sense of self-sufficiency. It's smaller things too. Like the ability to fix clogged plumbing or to handle woodland creatures who have sneaked, or been carried, inside the house.

I, for instance, am unfazed when my cats play mouse hockey on the bedroom floor, whether the furry puck is dead or alive. My dog, a PBGV, and my two Siamese cats can be entertained for hours by staring at a baseboard heater behind which a small mammal is hiding. I find this terribly amusing, not scary, especially when Louis, the dog, tries to get the critter out with his tongue. This to me is better than watching Comedy Central.

Once I can catch the little interloper, back outside it goes (or into the trash if it's in a state of rigor mortis). I've removed a live and terrified chipmunk from the top of the curtain rod in my office, where he was staring down at me on my computer, blinking his little SOS eyes until I noticed him. I saved his toosh by swaddling him in the curtain and carrying him outside incognito, while the fixated (and I might add, not so smart) cats continued to stare hopefully at the curtain rod.

Likewise I've freed baby bunnies from the dog's jaws, thrown away a couple of stiff squirrel frisbees, and caught a garter snake in the kitchen with pasta tongs. This last one gave me the creeps big time, but I attribute this to our primordial human fears of falling and of snakes, supposedly inculcated into our brain cells as primitive defenses while we still slogged about in the ooze.

I've fixed toilets, patched walls, replaced five gallon bottles in the water cooler, put line switches on table lamps and installed a new hard drive in my computer. So I am always amazed, and a little disgusted, by the image of a woman standing on a chair and shrieking because there's a mouse in the house.

Women can be riveters, welders, airline pilots, give BIRTH for Pete's sake, and a little mouse scares them?

It seems so. My new honey (who I want in my life but don't need) has a mother who is apparently tough as nails. Raised her son alone, worked all her life, and, like me, fits the stereotype of a high performance woman: Someone who can go from zero to bitch in 2.1 seconds. Yet when she found a mouse in her apartment she called her son to come and remove it.

He had to take three trains to get from Queens to Rockaway, a two-hour one way trip, to catch the offender. When he got there, turns out the mouse was caught and dead under a pot in the kitchen sink.

"Let me get this straight," he said to his mother in exasperation. "You made me come all this way to throw away a DEAD MOUSE?"

"Of course I did. You didn't think I was gonna do it?" she asked. "It scares me."

Is she really that scared? Or did she just want her son to feel needed? You'd think, maybe, that wildlife in Rockaway is an anomaly, but it's not. There's a nature preserve there that is home to Texas jackrabbits, definitely not indigenous. They're probably descended from visiting lagomorphs who escaped from JFK Airport and hopped on over to their new Rockaway home. (You have a better theory?)

Where I live, indigenous wildlife is part of the most docile suburban scene. Turtles, skunks, raccoons, red foxes, deer, chipmunks, squirrels, mice, even coyotes, are all regularly spotted (but usually not indoors). Not to mention wild birds, for whom we shlep home 20 and 40 pound bags of nuts and seeds to fill our feeders with.

Between toting heavy bags of bird food, domestic pet rations and groceries for humans, not to mention grass seed, lime, manure, mulch and wood chips for our lawns and gardens (and milorganite to keep the deer away), Lewisboro women are building muscles and moxie.

Not that I'm working toward the obsolescence of men (although the thought has crossed my mind when I'm in "high performance" mode). I like having my honey around, and besides he's a really good kisser. But if I could just lift my TV alone and not have to rush to the chiropractor, or install my air-conditioner on my own, I'd be very happy. Right now it's, "I'm the weaker sex, hear me groan." I'd much prefer, "I am woman, hear me roar."

Too Hot to Handle

Forget sex. Forget money. There's something that couples fight about even more, something that I think is a much better measure of compatibility: Temperature.

Think about it. How many couples do you know where he likes the air conditioning on in the car, and she'd rather have the windows open and feel the breeze on a hot day? Or she likes it cool at night, maybe even with a window cracked, preferring to snuggle under a down comforter, and he would rather have the heat cranked into the 70's?

Or how about agreeing on the appropriate temperature to serve food? I like a cup of tea that is steaming hot, yet I prefer to eat solid foods that can be served at room temperature or cooler (like salads and appetizer-y stuff). At least my ex and I were compatible when it came to food, so he was a joy to cook for, but I know a lot of guys who like food so hot they have to gasp for cooling sips of air between their scalding mouthfuls.

I have seen battles over the thermostat that rival the antics in the film, "War of the Roses." I'm not mentioning any names, but in one house, *he* turns the air-conditioning down to frigid, and the second he leaves for work, *she* turns it back up so she can stay in her sleeveless dresses during the day. In another marriage (now ended), *she* put the heat on in the car, *he* opened the moon roof.

For every man or woman that likes it hot, there's a mate that will too. But discovering temperature preferences is a challenge, as the subject is an extremely delicate one. A woman would have little trouble articulating, "Faster and a little to the left," but she'll practically strangle on, "Could you please turn the heat up?" Likewise I've seen overdressed men sitting in restaurants, with sweat pouring down their faces, mopping their brows with their napkins, and telling their dinner dates that it's just that the food is too spicy.

The problem with this temperature problem is that we usually don't find out about each other's comfort levels until after we are living together. By then, we have discovered so much that is endearing about each other that we figure the hot and cold running differences are minor adjustments we'll have to adapt to.

Temperature preferences don't cause divorces, but they sure lead to arguments. In my opinion, constant bickering is no less destructive to a marriage than a cheating spouse who has the hots for his wife's best friend.

I think people need to tell each other these intimate requirements right up front, before they get too far into a relationship and then spend the rest of it skulking subversively around the thermostats. Acceptable temperature ranges should be part of prenuptial agreements.

Likewise, vacations should be planned in conjunction with meteorological input, so that a couple doesn't end up in the Florida Keys in August or Australia in December, unless they both enjoy sweltering heat. Right now, my friend and I are trying to make travel plans for this summer. *One* of us seems destined to go to Antarctica because the South of France, where the *other* one of us wants to go, is too hot. It's looking like we may stay home.

If we do, I'm not turning on the air-conditioning.

Alice in Dildoland

There it lay, bilious yellow with a lace of blue-green corrosion spreading up the shaft. My vibrating, multi-speed, battery operated, glow-in-the-dark dildo was dead. Now I would have to replace it. My panic set in.

I have never bought a dildo in my life. This one was a gift from my cousin Wanda, intended as a joke. Over the years, I'd grown to like it, a lot, and never even thought that one day it might die. As I disposed of it in the kitchen garbage, I began to consider my options. I could go to a store (I know there are such stores, although I don't know where), or buy through a mail order catalogue, but either way I'd have to talk to a live person, which mortified me. And I'm not even at the embarrassing part yet. Then I thought of another alternative, the perfect solution to my little problem: the Internet!

I am a reasonably proficient cyberbabe; I know my way around chat rooms and newsgroups and websites. Surely, there must be plenty of adult websites that had what I needed. Wasn't everybody fussing about the cornucopia of x-rated material on the net? That was just what I was looking for.

So I pointed my browser to search for online sex stores, and found tons of websites. It seemed easy enough. A dildo is a dildo, right? Wrong. Dildos are now called dongs. And the selection is mind-boggling. Now I had to decide what kind of dong I wanted.

My choices included life-like dongs, specialty dongs and better-than-real dongs. Life-like included double dongs, squirters, dongs with straps, smooth, veined, cut, uncut, vibrating and/or rotating. I don't know about you, but in my real life hardly any of these choices exist.

Okay, maybe squirters. A guy who could do all this stuff would be really, really popular in my neighborhood.

Specialty dongs (as if life-like weren't special enough) included jellies—clear plastic phalluses in candy colors that were touted as being "so alive you'll fall in love at first touch," fuzzy soft-skinned dongs, and butt plugs. No thank you. That orifice is exit-only on my body.

Better-than-real seemed the best bet. Many of the dongs were made from molds of real guys, and one particularly attractive dong was called the Emperor. It came in two sizes, six inch and eight inch, and three colors, "flesh," "mulatto," and "black". Excuse me, but aren't mulatto and black both flesh tones? Why didn't they just call the Caucasian dong "whitey"? I realized that writing a letter of complaint off to the dong company wasn't going to end racism on the planet, and I would still be left dongless. So I swallowed my pride and got down to choosing.

I had read on one of the websites that women tend to have eyes bigger than their vaginas when it comes to buying dongs. This site advised women to find their ideal dong size by—I am NOT kidding—paring hard vegetables like zucchinis and carrots into different widths and lengths and experimenting. Yeah right. I remember reading that vaginas expand to accommodate the size of whatever's in them so I figured that an eight inch Emperor would be nice. Black. I mean, who doesn't love Denzel? I typed in my order and credit card number. I couldn't believe how expensive dongs are. I rationalized that if I used it for the rest of my life—every day—it would be a worthwhile investment.

By the end of the week, my package arrived. I took my dong to the bedroom for a road test. And I have to say that I don't think it's true that vaginas can expand to any size. My Emperor did not fit. Even with water-soluble lubricant, it wasn't budging. And it seemed to be allergic to the lubricant; the dark skin was peeling off in patches. It looked like it had that skin disease Michael Jackson claims to have, vitiligo. Clearly I was going to have to exchange this thing. Oh God.

I called the number on the invoice, and a whisky-voiced man with a Southern accent answered.

"Um, hi," I said. "I bought an Emperor from you and it, um, seems to be defective."

"Defective? Why that's our most popular model. Which one was it, the six or eight inch?"

"Eight."

"That's a really nice one. Lifelike isn't it?"

"Well, uh, I guess. Doesn't look like anyone I've known."

"What's the matter with it?"

"It's peeling. The rubber is coming off on the, uh, scrotum, and it looks awful."

"I'm surprised. That's the highest quality latex you can buy."

"Maybe this is just a bad one."

"Did you use it? We can't take used merchandise back."

"Oh, of course not!" I didn't tell him why.

"Well, ship it back to us and we'll send you a new one."

"Can I get a six inch this time? I didn't realize how big this would be."

"Yeah, the circumference on that baby is pretty amazing huh?" he chuckled. "Sure, you just write what you want on a note and put it to my attention. Name's Ed."

"Okay Ed, thanks."

Soon after, my replacement dong arrived, six inches long as requested, and narrower. But this one had a suction cup at its base. I tried to imagine what for. Seems I can operate a computer but, in my opinion, and undoubtedly Ed's, I am clueless when it comes to sex aids. I plunked the dong down on the dresser while I pondered my dilemma. No way was I calling Ed again.

Well, the dong is still stuck to my dresser. And I thought I was embarrassed before. I think I'll just leave it there. I could use it to hold my bracelets. I've learned one thing from this: Dongs, like vegetables, should be bought in person. Now I need to find the right disguise so I can go shopping. Maybe I can find a cool wig on the Internet.

Roos, Vhy Vass I in da Hospital?

There's no question that we baby boomers are aging. I can blame my forgetfulness on the car accident that scrambled my brain and short-circuited my memory. But nearly everyone about my age is just as forgetful. The so-called "normal" population. This is truly scary.

I was at an inn recently and a couple who admitted to being in their forties hauled a tackle box to the breakfast table. It contained their vitamins. I take vitamins too, and minerals, and all kinds of herbs that are supposed to be good for me. Gingko biloba, flaxseed, folic acid, calcium…I don't remember them all. But I don't need a tackle box when I travel. Yet.

One friend has a vitamin ritual. She takes each pill individually, with a deeply wished mantra preceding each swallow. "This is to make my bones strong," she intones for the calcium. "This is to help my hot flashes," she says for the black cohosh. "This is for my immune system," she repeats for the echinacea. When she gets to the gingko capsule, she often stares blankly, sometimes swallows it mantra-less. Gingko's for memory.

Another friend locked herself out of the house naked last week. Fortunately she was on her portable phone, so she hid in a bush and called a friend to come and get her and clothe her. My sister-in-law loses her car keys nearly every day. She thinks she has Alzheimer's, but a friend in her seventies tells us if you can wake up in the morning and say Alzheimer's, you don't have it.

The things I do are pretty bad too. Like, I find my coffee mug in the linen closet, the mug I looked for hours and gave up on. Or I leave the oven on with a chicken pot pie in it, for four hours. I actually did something my father used to do and I used to howl at, when I was six. I ran all over a store looking for my sunglasses. I swore I had set them down next to the peanut butter doggie treats. Insisted I had, asked the clerk if he could move the display aside to find my glasses.

"The glasses that are on top of your head, ma'am?" Yeah, those. Duh. And me, a "Ma'am?" It's not so funny now.

But I am not as bad as my dear departed stepmother. Yet. Omi, as my kids called her, was a regal German woman with a thick accent. She came to this country to escape World II and worked as a governess for a prominent New York City family. She was often mistaken as the mother of her charges because she was so sure of herself. She didn't marry my father until she was 72 and he was 68. She seduced him actually.

When she was in her eighties, we didn't stay in regular phone contact. She lived in California with my dad, I was in New York raising babies. But we always had a psychic connection, and knew when something was wrong with the other. So one day I called her, disturbed.

"Mom, are you all right? I've been worried about you and I don't know why."

"*Neu ja,*" she replied, "I'm fine. I just got back from da hospital."

"THE HOSPITAL! Why were you in the hospital?"

I heard her call out to Ruth, a day nurse who looked after my father and apparently my stepmother too.

"Roos, vhy vass I in da hospital?" Pause.

"*Ach ja.* I had breast cancer."

Fortunately, she didn't die of breast cancer. She swore that the full glass of vodka she drank every evening had preserved her, although I have my doubts about that. I believe it was her loving approach to life. She lived to be 86 and died of plain old age.

I'm gonna keep taking my gingko, not that it will help my damaged axons. And my new mantra, when I am really forgetful is to repeat Omi's question: "Roos, vhy vass I in da hospital?" Feel free to make it your own. It sure helps you laugh at this aging process. What else are we gonna do? As another friend's mom says, "The alternatives are not so appealing."

So, Was It Good for Me?

You've read about it everywhere, seen ads, heard stories, watched TV shows dedicated to its marvels. The little blue pill that makes magic. Viagra.

When my doctor suggested I try it, I was surprised.

"But I'm a girl!" I blurted.

"Yes, I know that Julietta," she said. "It's fairly obvious. But a study I read shows it helps women too."

How, you wonder, did I get into this pickle? Ya got me. A combination of being an aging baby boomer and panic meds, most likely. Or the stress of moving, divorcing, and coping with chronic pain from a car accident. Or all of the above. In any case, my frustration levels were exceeding my libido levels.

"Just try it," said the doc. ""I'll give you three samples, you'll break them in half, so if there are any side effects, they'll be minimal."

"SIDE EFFECTS? What kind of side effects? I have a panic disorder. I don't do side effects."

"Yes, I know you have a panic disorder Julietta. That's why I see you, remember? You're not going to die from Viagra."

"You swear?"

"I swear. Your blood pressure may drop, and you might get a headache."

"But my blood pressure is already so low it's practically pediatric. If it drops I'll be dead."

"No, you just may have a 'gray-out.' But it won't matter, you'll be lying down anyway."

"Sounds great," I said sarcastically, wondering if having an orgasm was really worth this much anxiety.

"Well, the idea is you won't be focusing on your blood pressure. Besides, it goes up during sex, not down. You'll be fine."

I couldn't wait to rush home with my samples and play. I felt like I'd just been sent home with the mythical Spanish fly. Illicit, sexy, thrilling. I broke a pill in half, swallowed it with water and sat down to read the package insert, as I had promised the doc I would. As soon as I got to the contraindications part, my heart began to pound. I saw "...risk of death with history of cardiac problems...fatal stroke...should not be used by women..." and the list went on. Maybe it was the Viagra, or maybe it was an incipient panic attack, but I was feeling really woozy.

I must be nuts, I thought, to take one drug that kills my libido, and another one to bring it back. Why take either? What ever happened to all-natural, to the crunchy granola, 'twigs, bark and foo-foo shit' days? Now I was a guinea pig for sex. I was certain I was going to die. I called my doctor.

Her machine answered.

"I am having a panic attack, I feel awful, like I am going to pass out. I think you better call me right away. I'm terrified."

Ten minutes later, still light-headed, I called again.

"I'm not having fun. I am really scared." I rambled on at some length, naming all the reasons I should not be taking Viagra and wanting to know how long it would stay in my body. "And on top of it all, my face is the color of six beets right now. Call me!"

I then called a friend who's a therapist. I told her what I'd done.

"Why are you calling me then? You should be playing some sexy music and seeing if the Viagra works. Don't waste time. It peaks at around an hour. Put on some Celine Dion or something."

"Celine Dion? You must be kidding. She makes me want to drown. How about some Marvin Gaye?"

"Put on whatever the hell you want, but stop talking to me. You are not gonna die. No man in my practice has ever died from taking it, you won't either. Those cardiac warnings are for 375 pound men getting laid for the first time after a heart attack."

"But what about women in your practice?"

"They're all dying to get their hands on it. You should consider yourself lucky."

"You know, that was a *really* poor choice of words."

"Oh, you know what I mean. Women really want to try it, they think it's unfair that pharmaceutical companies care more about male libido. Now quit wasting time and enjoy yourself before you miss the peak."

Understand that my libido was probably at an all-time low at this point, and my anxiety level at a record high. And my face felt like T minus zero, ready for blastoff. Still, I got out my toys, my Discman and prepared to get down and get funky. Then the phone rang.

"You are not dying, Julietta," said my doctor. "If you were dying you would not have been able to make so many phone calls."

"But my face is red, I feel really weird. What's going on with me?"

"I dunno," she said. "Could be the blood is going to the wrong zone. Maybe if you rub your nose, you'll come."

"Ha ha."

"Quit obsessing and go do sex. I want a full report."

So, I climbed into bed, earphones on my head and equipment in hand. I listened to my new CD, Moby's *Play* (I couldn't find Marvin, and my time was running out; anyway, the Moby title seemed apt). Instead of experiencing pleasure, I worried. And whenever I tried to focus on just letting go, my brain skunked me with one repetitive thought: Bob Dole, Bob Dole, Bob Dole, Bob Dole.

Maybe he gets Liddy's rocks off, but not mine. The Viagra spokesmodel was a very unwelcome intrusion into my sexual fantasies. I was about to give up altogether when suddenly, without warning, I peaked and crashed. It was like the sound of a car driving by really fast—you hear it coming and going, and then all is quiet. That's when I realized I had a bad headache.

I laughed hysterically, thrilled to have survived and bummed that I had just missed what was supposed to be the best damn orgasm I should ever have had. This Viagra may work wonders on men, but as usual, the mysteries of the female anatomy and psyche have not been unraveled sufficiently to assist in producing nirvana, or anything close.

Is it good for us? Heck no. The most recent studies (the ones my doctor read after my sexual escapade) show Viagra doesn't work in women. And if we do decide to take Viagra anyway, hoping against hope that it will work, we'll probably end up saying to our partners, "Not again honey. Now I *really* have a headache."

There are other things to take to boost libido and orgasm, like testosterone or prostaglandin gel or amino acid supplements, but nothing without side effects. And there's nothing yet that is the female equivalent of the magic blue pill that can be taken before sex, focuses on The Zone, gets you off, and leaves the body. So until we get our hands on some really good stuff, we're going to have to have our orgasms the old-fashioned way, earn them.

Halfway to Alte Kokkerdom

My new realtor sat across from me, sweat dampening her blouse. It was, according to the "heat index", whatever the heck that is, well over a hundred degrees outside. I'd come into her office primarily to use the ladies room, and to enjoy a brief respite in air conditioning. Next thing I knew, I was looking at the condo book.

In a million years I never would have thought that I'd consider living in Heritage Hills, a nearby retirement community. Planned community my ass. To me it was a close cousin to Leisure World where my aging parents used to live, that my Dad used to call Seizure World. My father used to swear to me that they did a body count there every morning to see who was left. I thought Heritage Hills was a place for *alte kokkers*, not swinging singles or young families. You can imagine my reluctance to think about living there.

"Honey," said my new realtor, "face it. It's the graying of America. We baby-boomers are aging in a big wave. I closed on five of these units yesterday. Five! They are selling like hotcakes. And not to senior citizens. People our age and younger. With little kids even. These places will only become more popular as we get older."

I was shaken. Bad enough being single, having to worry about condoms again, let alone condos. Bad enough having to move to someplace new after almost 20 years of privacy in the woods. But a retirement village? With a golf course?

I went home and called a friend. The tears were knocking at my eyelids. She and I had been discussing the availability of rentals (practically nil) and their attributes (mostly dumps) and their prices (inflated).

"I'M GONNA HAVE TO BUY A CONDO. A CONDO!!" I wailed. "No more privacy, and I'll have wall-to-wall carpets instead of hardwood floors," I shouted. "And Harvest Gold colored appliances. This is the death of my aesthetic life!"

"Babydoll," she said dryly, "get a grip. We're halfway to *alte kokkerdom*, remember? Those units are beautiful, lots of them are private, and you can change the appliances and the carpeting. And there are so many people there who might adopt you as a daughter."

"What if they want to date me, not adopt me?" I asked, thinking of my single pals who are man magnets now, and not attracting true North material, if you catch my drift. More like ironing filings or metal shavings. The dregs.

"Hey, maybe you'll find somebody rich with a heart condition. A little Viagra and you could be an heiress."

"Quit teasing. This is serious."

"So am I," she said. "Just think, no more lawn to mow, no more snow plow bills, you'll have a jitney to the train, access to exercise classes, lots of pools, and central air conditioning."

Ah, pools. Air conditioning. Good points. The heat has gotten to me. I'm snappish, cranky and sweaty. And sick of hiding in my bedroom, the only room in my house with an air conditioner.

"Not to mention, "she continued, "that great bagel place in the shopping center, Jaipore Indian restaurant is a stone's throw away, Dinardo's farm has THE best butter and sugar corn around, and the town of Katonah's a five minute drive."

"Yeah," I chirped. "And…the supermarket sells freshly made Krispy Kreme donuts. The only place around other than Starbucks, which marks them up 200%."

"There you go. If you see one you like (condo, not donut), snap it up baby! Grab it!"

So, maybe I'll grab. I can almost see myself now. I'll remodel. I'll learn to walk a dog and pick up poo. I'll learn to be neighborly. I'll take a yoga class, maybe even join the opera club. Maybe I could sneak into the pool at night for a skinnydip. Or I could learn to play golf. If Gerald Ford could do it, I certainly could. Even if I end up looking more like Chevy Chase's version of Gerald Ford.

Just know one thing: I may be halfway to *alte kokkerdom*, but if I buy a condo, I'll be right next to the Krispy Kreme donuts. And that, I think, is the best reason to move there.

Lost and Found

On the same day that *NYPD Blue* aired an episode in which some poor schmuck gets his willie lopped off, my friend Don was under the knife for prostate cancer. It was a day full of the ironic and unexpected, the least of which was a snowstorm that socked the Northeast and froze the feet of Don's wife who, in her altered mental state, wore open clogs to the hospital.

It's fair to say that no one's mental state was very stable in the weeks preceding Don's surgery. Cancer will do that to you. So will the fact that men who undergo surgery for prostate cancer have only a 60% chance of regaining erectile function. Or the fact that every man, if he lives long enough, will develop prostate cancer.

Although this kind of cancer, if treated, is rarely fatal, the thought of knives anywhere near male genitalia is enough to cause shrinkage. Just try saying "vasectomy" to a guy and see what I mean. I bet there are even men who would choose slow death and no surgery over the chance of never having a hard-on again.

Don, however, handled his medical crisis with grace and humor He became one of the most educated consumers (if surgery is a consumer item) of the pros and cons of seeding with radioactive pellets, radiation, chemotherapy, and cutting. It was he who brought up the erectile function issue and asked me (okay, I prodded) if I wanted to be kept apprised of his post-surgery progress.

"Hell yeah!" I said. "The whole neighborhood does!"

"Maybe I should put up a sign," he said. "Like those thermometers that measure donations."

"But, of course, it wouldn't be a thermometer," I said. "It would be a big plywood penis with lines showing degrees of elevation."

"Gives new meaning to the term 'E-meter'," he laughed.

"It could go from zero at the bottom, and at 180 degrees it would say 'Don gives himself a black eye'."

We agreed that on E-day, we'd have a party. Maybe a Maypole dance.

This was funny, but it wasn't. I mean, what if…?

For his surgery, Don had chosen New York's finest docs, but their names gave him a jolt. The cutter was Doctor Sawchuck, the neurologist Dr. Wiener. Yes, really. His wife liked the neurologist because he wore the same clogs she had on. Any reassurance in the storm.

Well, these guys knew what they were doing, The day after surgery, Don's wife called me to tell me all was well and both sets of nerves had been spared.

"Meaning?"

"Meaning, Don will live to boink again. And more importantly, the cancer is gone." To me, that alone was cause for celebration.

Meanwhile, big controversy over the *NYPD Blue* hit the media, not only because of the severed johnson. Seems the victim's watch had gone missing too, and the fire department was to blame. News-folks were squeamish, grossed out by the dismemberment, and were also reporting that the New York Fire Department had gone ballistic that anyone should think they'd steal a Rolex. Nevermind that the show's producer said the story was based on fact.

Me, I'd be more worried about a losing a willie than a watch. Different strokes for different folks, I guess. But if you live in New York City and are a fan of *NYPD Blue*, you better hope your apartment doesn't catch fire.

Floyd Joy, Floyd Joy, Floyd Joy

I've lived through hurricanes before, since I moved to the New York City suburbs 27 years ago. I've endured fear, crashing trees, spinning deck furniture, demented wind chimes, and temporarily psychotic pets.

I even got married during a hurricane—little votive candles all over our house, the rabbi backlit by a roaring fire, two violinists playing Bach concertos, and a percolator heating coffee to accompany the wedding cake, thanks to my johnny-on-the spot landlord who converted his tractor into a generator. The toilets didn't flush since the electric pumps were *kaput*, but our guests didn't seem to mind. They still say it was a memorable and beautiful wedding.

Luckily, I've been spared the loss of family, friends or pets as a result of a storm. Others who endure these disasters are not all so fortunate. But I've just lost stuff, if I've lost anything at all, and stuff is just not really that important to me. Floyd was the first time a tropical storm made me laugh. The name alone is enough to make you chortle.

My amusement started when I heard the storm was headed our way. I don't know about you, but I have several male friends who get excited at the thought of really bad weather. I mean get excited in a way that I find, well, a little peculiar. Their eyes glaze over, their breath comes faster and they can't stay away from the weather channel. If lightning is blazing and cracking and thunder is shaking the house, these guys open the front door, stand on the porch and are mesmerized.

"Wow."

"Yeah. Did you see that one?"

"Oh man. Far out."

I haven't heard this kind of talk since a Jefferson Airplane Concert in 1969. One of these friends once gave my then-husband a CD, *Thunderstorm Terror*, for his birthday. A sound effects CD. If we played it, the pets had the good sense to hide under the bed. Needless to say, the husband sat on the couch in the dark and listened to it as if it were the Moonlight Sonata. The movie *Twister* was a "must-own", the flying cow and double funnels replayed over and over again. I think the husband thought of changing careers to become a hurricane chaser. There were days I wished he had.

So the concerned calls start coming in, from these penis-people who were all atwitter about Floyd. Put the lawn furniture in the garage, they warned. Bring in the hanging plants. Lock up the pets (they were already in hiding). Better tie down anything under five foot one. This last bit of advice a reference to my diminutive stature. Ha ha.

The wind chimes began clanging and gonging, and with everything tucked away and all the windows closed, I decided to take a nap. I woke up in the dark to the sound of rain slashing my windows and trees careening in the wind, and I went down to check the basement.

I began cursing. There was an inch of water covering a third of the basement carpet, slowly creeping its way across the room. I cursed some more. Then I called the would-be hurricane chaser and informed him of the flood. His reaction was anger, as if I were somehow responsible for preventing this, as if I could have been more vigilant to keep Floyd at bay. He began cursing. Then he agreed to come over and help. When he got to my house, he cursed some more.

The first thing we discovered was that my sump pump had rusted out. We didn't learn this, however, until we'd vacuumed the first barrelful of water, which then burst out of the bottom of the pump as we lifted it. More cursing ensued.

Hurricane Chaser got angrier, and began to push the water out of the basement with an aluminum snow shovel. I found this humorous, the shoveler did not. So I disappeared upstairs to make phone call after phone call to locate a sump pump or shop vac somewhere in my vicinity. No luck. Finally on the advice of a friend, I called the fire department, because they do pumping in emergencies.

An hour later, two fire trucks arrived, red lights flashing like we were a crime scene. By this time, my basement shoveler was shirtless, dripping sweat, red in the face and releasing torrents of expletives to match Floyd's stormy downpour.

I heard the voices of the newly arrived manly-men and then a busy flurry of activity. I crept downstairs to see three men in brown rain slickers and fire hats, fluorescent tape proclaiming them to be Fire Department volunteers. These men, accompanied by the hurricane-chasing wannabe, were doing the Goldens Bridge version of the flat foot floogie, using brooms to sweep, yes sweep, the water out of my basement.

"So, this is the high-tech pumping service the Fire Department offers?" I queried.

"Well ma'am, to tell ya the truth, the water's not deep enough for our pumps."

And, to be honest, I'm glad the water wasn't that deep. But I could not contain my laughter. I went back upstairs to call a friend, and we laughed hysterically at the feeble attempts of these men in uniform to keep nature at bay.

After a frustrating half-hour of brooms versus water (the Sorcerer's Apprentice comes to mind here), one of the firemen asked if he could use the phone. He called home and asked if his shop vac was there. When he got an affirmative answer, he told his roommate a neighbor would be over to pick it up.

This is why I like living in a small community. The firefighters are your neighbors, and they're really sincere about helping out.

The firefighters left to go on another call. Floods and fires and downed trees abounded. Our problem was literally just a weensy drop in the bucket that Floyd was filling. We got the shop vac and started sucking up water. What we hadn't counted on was Louis, the dog who sings.

As soon as he heard the whine of the shop vac's motor, Louis thought he'd been cued for his solo. He "aroooooooo-ed" while we vacuumed the water out of the basement. Somewhere during that serenade, Hurricane Man regained his sense of humor.

"You know," he said, "it's only water." Duh. Like I hadn't known this all along. "And the carpet looks better than when we spent all that money to have it steam cleaned."

"Yup," I said. "Plus it's rainwater, so natural, so, uh, gentle...so free!"

That rainwater caused an awful lot of damage. It ruined buildings, businesses and cars in my community. My heart goes out to those who have lost stuff. But it's only stuff, and I'm sure this community will rally around its shopkeepers and residents to help them out, just like our firefighter neighbor helped us. And I'm really grateful that all Floyd did to me was clean my carpet.

Phobobabes

It's three in the morning, my heart is pounding, my palms are sweaty, my mouth is dry. The irrational part of my brain is screaming inside my head, "Def Con one! Def Con one! We are having a heart attack! Call the ambulance! Go to the emergency room!"

The rational part of me is rolling its eyes and saying, "Aw jeez, here we go again. Hello? Wouldja calm down? This is a panic attack. You've had them since you were six years old. You're not dying. Can we please go back to sleep now?"

But if you are like me, one of approximately 10 to 15% of adults who suffer from an anxiety-based disorder, you know that sleep is impossible. A panic attack, a full body reaction to something as simple as a thought or a heart palpitation, is literally a reflex, something out of the mind's control. Hormones gone amok. Sometimes they seem to just come out of nowhere.

According to an article in *the New York Times Magazine*, the research says we're apparently hardwired this way, usually because of some traumatic event early in life. The brain reacts once in that "fight or flight" response—to a snake, to being stuck in an elevator, to getting lost in the supermarket—and the neurons learn that twisted, tortured path to hell-on-earth forever more. Each time we think we're in danger, kaboom! A chemical chain reaction is set off, primal and survivalist.

And we phobics think we're in danger a lot, because we're great thinkers. Very imaginative. We can visualize a plane bursting into flames and crashing to the earth just from seeing an airline commercial. We picture our cars leaping the guardrail of the Tappan Zee Bridge if we have to drive over it. We're afraid of being somewhere without access to a bathroom. Our lists of terror-inducing activities are extensive. Many of us are so paralyzed by fear we can't go to movies, or restaurants, or in extreme cases, to work.

Plenty of phobics are famous. Aretha Franklin, John Madden, Whoopi Goldberg and Gene Shalit are all afraid to fly. Willard Scott is afraid of public speaking. Then there's the lesser-known phobics like me and my niece Sadie (who have an unofficial club called "Phobobabes") and all the folks I meet online at three in the morning when I am sure I am going to die, and there's no one I feel I can call to talk me down. It's too late to phone anyone in New York or California, and if I do force myself to call, I am usually horribly embarrassed the next day when the crisis has passed. Very few people understand what living with a panic disorder is like. So we phobics stick together, sometimes in the strangest ways.

I think a great solution when you're short-circuiting on panic is to turn on the computer and sign on to America Online. There, Psych Online and Sigmund's Sitting Room are just two mouse-clicks away. Even in the wee hours, the chat room is hopping, full to the brim with Siggie's regulars and irregulars. I'm greeted right away.

Phobo1: "Hi Apple, what's up?"

Applejax: "Oh God, help. I'm freaking out. I'm having a panic attack."

Phobo1: "U r okay honey. Just breathe. Nice and slow."

Applejax: "I can't. Too scared. Fingers numb. Heart pounding. I think it's a heart attack."

Nursiepoo: "U r hyperventilating is all. It's not a heart attack. This ever happen before?"

Applejax: "Lots. Since I was little. Oh God, I am so scared."

JesusluvsU: "Apple do not take the name of our Lord in vain! Show some respect."

Phobo1: "Lay off her Jesus, she's having a panic attack."

Nursiepoo: "Got any Xanax, Apple?"

Applejax: "Ativan. Took it 10 minutes ago."

Nursiepoo: "Good. It'll kick in any minute. Plus we'll distract u."
JesusluvsU: "Trust in Jesus, Apple, He'll guide u through this."
Applejax: "Jesus u r really working this Jewgirl's nerves. SHUT UP!
Phobo1: U go girlfriend! Now u r distracted! Feeling better?"
Applejax : "No, I'm afraid I'm going to die."
Phobo1: "How many of these have u had in your life Apple? If u r like me, hundreds, right? And they all felt just like this. But u didn't die, and u r not going to this time."
Applejax: "U sure?"
Phobo1: "Pretty sure, yes. Try this. Type what I type."
Applejax: "Huh?"
Phobo1: "Type what I type."
Applejax: "Type what I type."
Phobo1: "That's it."
Applejax: "That's it."
Phobo1: "Now take nice, slow breaths in. Let the air out between pursed lips."
Applejax: "Now take nice, slow....wait, am I supposed to be typing or breathing?"
Phobo1: "Both."
Nursiepoo: "Apple, drugs working yet?"
Applejax: "I think so, I'm getting sleepy. Thank God. Oops, don't start Jesus, okay?.... Listen guys, thanks. I'm going to go to bed now."
Phobo1: "Okay, but we're here if u need us."
Applejax: "Thx u. What topic did I interrupt anyway?"
Nursiepoo: "MPD."
Applejax: "MPD? What's that?"
Nursiepoo: "Multiple personality disorder. Jesus has eight."
Applejax: "Eight what? Personalities?"
JesusluvsU: "Yeppers."
Applejax: "Well good night, then. ALL of u. And thx."
Suddenly, sleep seems very, very appealing and not at all impossible.

Rage Against the Machine

The phone rings once, twice. And then, The Machine picks up.

Now listen folks, The Machine has been around long enough that we all know what The Machine is about. It answers the phone if a) you're not home b) you're busy or c) you're screening your calls and waiting to hear who it is to see if you'll pick up d) you have caller ID and don't feel like answering the friggin' phone. That's it.

The only information I need to know is did I call the right number. Right now, there are two schools of thought on this—the Number Givers and the Name Givers. Either way, I'll know if I have the right number if you tell me just one of those things. And your pre-programmed robot lady telling me "We-are-unable-to-come-to-the-phone-right-now…." does not help me. I need a name or a number, okay? I understand some of you can't program The Machine any better than you know how to program your VCR. Please get help.

When I get The Machine, I do not need to know that you're out ferrying kids to soccer or that you're busy in the garden or that you *might* be washing your hair, or that you're not home (something I think is really stupid to tell anyone who calls, especially if you give your name AND number—that's like saying, "Here's where I live, come steal my stuff) or that I've reached So-and-So's answering machine and if I would leave a message with my name and number and brief message and time of my call, you'll call back.

Well, DUH! We all have lives, we're all busy, and I think we all know why The Machine picks up. And I think we all know what to do, and we ought to let The Machine do what it's best at, which by the way, usually includes recording the time of the call.

I've heard some great outgoing messages, like, "If you didn't call 555-1234, you have the wrong number." Or, "Hi, this is 555-1234, and it's the 90's. You know what to do." (Have you noticed in all the movies, phone numbers start with "555" so that we, the public, won't be foolish enough to actually call a number we hear in a film, thinking we're going to reach the real Will Hunting or something? Jeez Louise. But see, I had to do it above, so you don't go calling someone real. I apologize.)

If you're going to leave *War and Peace* on your outgoing message, for the love of God, would you leave a code to bypass it and just let me leave you a message? Like, "If you don't want to hear my schedule for the next month and hear me count the reasons why I am unable to answer my phone, press 1 and the pound sign now to just leave a message." And really, is there anyone left on the planet who doesn't know what the pound sign is?

Gone are the days, I hope, when you don't know when to leave your message (after the beep, okay?) or you don't know if it's live or The Machine (Yeah, I know there's still some of you jokers out there whose outgoing message says "Hello?" with that little rise of the voice at the end, so you fake people out. Ha ha. Very funny.) And I hope that you all agree with me that The Machine is meant to take messages, not perpetuate terminal phone tag. So if you call me, please don't say, "Call me back. I have something REALLY important to tell you." Tell me why you called. I don't care how long the incoming message is if it's got the information I need. After all, it will save me a return call, and save me from the possibility of getting The Machine at your house.

Hair Today, Gone Tomorrow

What IS it with men and their hair?

Maybe it's only single men, who don't have anyone living with them to say, "You are not really going to go out like that are you?" A wife or partner would say something like that. They'd need to, to avoid profound public embarrassment. But then again, I also know married men with really bad hair issues.

There are actually men who think their hair looks fine if the color's turned brassy orange, if gray roots are showing, if it's combed over their bald spot from one ear to the other, if they use Rogaine and have peach fuzz on top of their head, if they have hairpieces, if they have hair plugs.

I try to imagine how these disgraceful things happen. Are men that clueless? Are their friends not telling them the truth about how they look?

A woman could ask her friend, "How do I look in this skirt?" and her friend would say, "Your butt looks big."

But if Bob asks Joe, "How does my hair look?" Joe would probably say "Huh?" Or, "Fine." Not that Bob would ask, mind you.

Women have learned not to listen to, "You look fine." "Fine" is one of the worst things a partner could say. Guaranteed a woman will change her clothes if she hears, "fine."

So listen guys, here's a heads-up: You need to "buy a vowel" in the hair department!

Generally speaking, bald is sexy. Gray is sexy (but keep it cropped short if you don't have a full head of hair). A hairpiece NEVER, I mean never ever, looks good. And in case you think no one can tell, you're wrong. Same with dyed hair. If you insist on coloring your hair, go to a professional. Most men who do home jobs get the color wrong, usually too dark. But even when it's professionally colored, we can tell—especially when your gray chest hairs are popping out of your collar.

Combovers are one of the stupidest styles ever. All those thin, sticky strands clinging pathetically to the top of your head, and one gust of wind and the whole follicular army stands at ridiculous attention. Better you should cut it short and buy a hat.

And plugs. Oy. It is impossible to sit across from a man with hairplugs and not look at them. You want to get a pencil and connect the dots, you want to know did it hurt to have those things stabbed into your head, you want to know who on earth thought a geometric grid would look natural, and where did that hair come from, anyway? Not to mention all those little crater-like scars that catch the light and make your head look like a lunar landscape.

Think Bruce Willis, Al Roker, ER's Anthony Edwards, Jesse Ventura, and Michael Jordan. Do NOT think Mike Wallace, Marv Albert, Sam Donaldson, or Zero Mostel. And if you have any doubts and your friends are no help, ask me. I'd be happy to tell you if your hair is making your head look bad.

Common Discourtesy

I've noticed that people are getting more impatient than ever. It's rampant. People become irritated when they have to stand in line. Professionals (and I use that term oh-so-loosely) that fall under the "customer service" umbrella are particularly snotty.

A perfect example is my local supermarket. Calling it "super" is a stretch. Okay: My local grocery store. Here, it's called the A and P. In California it'd be a Ralph's or a Safeway. In Florida, a Publix. You get the idea. Now, this is not my favorite place in the world to begin with. The produce is often stale, or moldy, or "coming in on the next truck." The parking situation at the shopping center has become a disaster since they remodeled and gave us a post office with a fake brick façade and plastic siding. You'd think the parking lot had been designed by the same monkeys that, if put on typewriters, would eventually, randomly, type all the works of Shakespeare.

Maybe if the designers had worked on their plan a wee bit longer, we'd have had enough room to get in and out of parking spaces without taking our lives in our hands, and without having to look in both directions for oncoming traffic instead of just one. I liked it when the parking was diagonal and one way. I thought it was safer. Call me a Luddite.

And I'm not the only one who thinks the parking lot is a disaster and that a tanning salon and a nail place are ridiculous additions to our hamlet. The town of Goldens Bridge needs these "improvements" like the Village of Katonah needs another antique store. Four out of five shoppers agree. I know, because I've asked them. Or heard them cursing loudly in the parking lot.

But the worst part is having to stand in a checkout line at the "Wee Wee," as my kids have called the A and P since they were small. I think it started when they were seven and four, and thought that saying "A and Pee Pee" was just about the nastiest, most disgusting toilet humor going. It evolved into the "Wee Wee" and has stuck.

"Mom," says my college-aged daughter, "I'm driving to the Wee Wee. Need anything?"

So, standing on line at the Wee Wee is an experience in dehumanization. Cashiers talk back and forth over customers' heads, usually about dates and binge drinking the night before, and don't even acknowledge us. No one even asks, "Paper or plastic?" anymore.

When the groceries are tallied, no one has ever stated out loud to me the exact amount that I owe, like, "That will be two thousand dollars and sixty cents, ma'am."

Instead, the cashiers stare off into space, or keep talking as if we shoppers don't exist, and expect us to intuit the amount of our purchases, or be able to read it on the weensy little LCD display above the register. This assumes we haven't been blinded by the laser UPC reader, or aren't middle-aged and can actually see the LCD display. So I always have to ask, "How much do I owe?"

I think the only words spoken to me recently by a cashier at the Wee Wee were, "Exact amount?" when I was writing a check. But Wee Wee customers are a much more friendly lot.

We gab to each other, often complaining about the service, the long lines, the lack of inventory that they're supposed to stock, or the fact that none of us has ever made it through a line without some item being unmarked. Pretty exciting stuff, huh?

I approach waiting on lines as a form of new-age meditation. What choice do I have but to wait? So I think of all the hustle and bustle in my life—the ringing phones, the email to be answered, the bills to be paid, the driving around—and am thankful to stand still. I daydream. I enjoy the air-conditioning. I listen to other people kvetch. Or I enjoy the kind little human interactions that occasionally take place.

Recently a dear friend had "earned" two frozen turkeys from spending so much money at the Wee Wee, and he gave the extra one to another guy in line. The cashier was shocked. Such courtesy is definitely uncommon at other stores. This I know because of my recent fracas at one of the A and P's competitors, Gristedes.

I was on my weekly Krispy Kreme run, and got in line behind an elegant blue-eyed woman with gray hair swept up into a French twist. She was chattering in a thick German accent to the checkout boy, a hottie with a tan and an earring. Then she looked over and eyed my bag of donuts. One donut was in hand and on its way to my mouth already.

"Are those good?" she asked. "I've heard so much about them."

"Mrrph," I replied through my mouthful of Boston creme donut. (Do you know that since 1998 there have been bills in Massachusetts legislature to make the Boston Cream donut the official donut of the Commonwealth? They spell it *cream*, not creme. And *donut*, not doughnut. It's a big debate, which some legislators find frivolous. Imagine. But no matter how you spell it, it has not a drop of real cream, or anything dairy for that matter. Go figure.)

"I think I get some. What are the flavors, which one should I get?"

I swallowed and told her the glazed or the jelly donuts were best for beginners.

"Ach, jelly. That's more traditional don't you think?"

"Sure, go for it," I said, while the hottie packed up her stuff.

"Will you show me where they are?" she asked.

I pointed to the header right behind us. In doing so I noticed a woman who'd gotten behind me in line. Her hair was dyed and shellacked, her nails were long and painted, her glasses were big and gold, and she was stuffed into her black and white zebra striped clothes. Her painted lips looked like she'd been sucking on lemons.

She tsk-tsked loudly and rolled her heavily made up eyes over the fact that Frau Sweetiepie was leaving the line.

"Is this the right kind?" Frau Sweetiepie asked me, showing me a powdered blueberry concoction that was definitely not the right kind.

"No, let me show you," I said, and walked the two feet with her back to the Krispy Kreme case. Sourpuss snarled.

"Oh, lighten up lady. He hasn't even finished bagging her things!" I said to her. "We've got the threat of nuclear holocaust and Y2K hanging over our heads, and you've got your knickers in a knot over a one lousy donut."

I tried to get back into my place in line, while Frau Sweetiepie was paying the cashier, and I realized Sourpuss had pushed her cart up so far I couldn't fit. I squeezed back in and gave her cart a nudge with my left hip. She didn't get the hint.

"Could you please get your cart out of my ass?" I asked.

She didn't budge, and looked in the other direction. I shoved my hip harder into her cart, and it rolled back. She pushed it right up against me.

"Listen lady," I said. "Move your cart. There's no room for me here, and my ass isn't even that big."

"Well, that's a matter of opinion," she snorted.

I unwedged myself, whirled around, and stood face to face with her.

"Hey babe," I said maliciously, "I'm ready to drop trou right here and now and go cheek to cheek with you. But I'm telling you, unless you wear size 4 panties, and it sure doesn't look like you do, your ass is way bigger than mine. So move your damn cart already!"

She backed her cart up.

Hottie was laughing out loud as he handed Frau Sweetiepie her change. She grinned at me and said, "Good for you. Doesn't it feel great to do that every now and then?"

"It sure does," I agreed. "Now," I asked the cashier, "how much do I owe you? For seven, not six donuts, because as you know, I ate one already."

"Oh, I wish I could give them to you for free! You've made my day. This is the most fun I've had working here. You just said everything I wish I could sometimes."

"I think I should get one of those bumper stickers that say 'Mean people suck'," I said.

"I already have one," he said. "Have a great day. I mean it."

And I think he really did mean it.

Road Warriors

I really, really hate sports utility vehicles. And I even used to own one. It got 14 miles per gallon and I felt like it was going to tip over every time the wind blew. When I sold it, I had enough money to buy two regular cars. And put gas in both of them. But I don't hate SUVS because they are expensive, gas-guzzling pollution machines, although you'd think that would be reason enough. I hate them because they terrify me.

When I see an SUV, I see a machine four times more likely than a normal-size car to kill me if it crashes into me. At night I know I am being followed by or am facing an SUV because its headlights are thirty-nine inches high and blinding me as I try to see the road. And SUV drivers seem to be lulled by the "safety features" of their vehicles. They drive as if their cars give them magical powers which exempt them from accepted rules of the road, the rules the rest of us have to observe.

Let's be honest here about sports utility vehicles. WHAT sports? WHAT utilities? What "off-road" experiences do we offer here in the burbs? The only activity I see these potential death cars engaged in is shlepping. Since when is shlepping a sport? And what exactly does utility mean?

SUVs are taking over our roads, and seem to be outnumbering, if not overpowering, normal, get-me-to-the-train-station-and-back cars. Besides the ridiculously expensive Range Rover, Mercedes, Lexus, and Lincoln SUVs I've swerved away from, I have actually seen two humvees around town. Humvees! *Hallo? Ah-nuld?* Are we in some cinema verité movie and no one's told us about it yet?

I don't just hate the expensive SUVs. I hate them all. As far as I'm concerned, putting an untrained driver in an SUV is like putting Doris Day in a tank and turning her loose on Rodeo Drive. (My apologies to Doris. Maybe General Patton gave her lessons that I just don't know about. Somehow, though, I think not.)

If drivers feel they are safer in SUVs and insist on driving them, then they should be required to take special driver's education courses and get special licenses. Paul Newman made all his kids take driving courses at Skip Barber's Racing School in Old Lyme, Connecticut, just so they'd know how to be extra, extra careful under normal conditions. I think passing an SUV course to get an SUV license is a perfectly reasonable idea. But I am also one of those people who thinks it should be mandatory for parents to obtain licenses in order to raise children. Who am I to judge?

So please, if you drive an SUV, do me a favor. Don't kill me. If you see me driving along in my little car, don't run me off the road. I prefer my driving experiences to be on-road, where they're supposed to be.

The Electronic Version of Crack

Let me first say that I can stop any time I want to. I don't have to do it every day. Sometimes, I don't think about it for a whole week. And it's not like I *have* to bid on stuff online. It's just for recreation. Okay?

I guess it all started when I was looking for a hard-to-find orange crate label (I've collected these labels for years; I'm from California). I really wanted to find Pullman Porter. A friend told me I could buy obscure things on eBay and get great deals. She herself had purchased lots of stuff, including a Mercedes that she got at deep discount for a mere $39,000. To a writer, that's not a bargain, that's a year's salary if you're lucky. But she convinced me to go check out the site and register to become a user.

Once I'd signed in, gotten a user name and begun to search, I was in heaven. I typed in "crate labels," and found hundreds, including a lovely set of three vegetable crate labels with a Bronco Bustin' theme, so I bid on them. Then I narrowed my search to just "orange crate labels." That still yielded too many results, and anyway I owned most of them, so I tightened the search even more to "Black Americana." Pullman Porter was nowhere to be found, but somehow or other I ended up bidding on an Aunt Jemima cookie jar and matching spoon rest.

I did get the three cowboy crate labels, for just $15.00, and I was delirious when I saw I was the winning bidder. Fortunately, I was saved from myself by someone who outbid me on the Aunt Jemima kitchen tchotchkes. They were reproductions anyway.

Now I'd had a taste of the battle to win an item, and I yearned for the excitement of losing ground to another bidder only to regain it with a higher bid. To see your name in the high bidder's spot, with the magic red words, "Auction has ended" underneath, is a rush that's hard to come by legally.

As my friend Treacy put it when she won an auction (she joneses for "Dick, Jane and Spot" books from the 1950's), "My heart hammered like a junkie who had just scored a lid." I emailed her and asked her what a lid was, I'd forgotten. "Me too," she said. "Lemme ask the spousal unit; he was arrested for possession in 1972." His response was, "Why does Julietta want to know? Is she buying a lid?" He was disappointed to find out that I, instead, was bidding on a 1946 deck of "Old Maid" cards for Treacy for Hanukkah. Which, by the way, I won. For only $7.00. In pristine condition.

I also got my 22 year old son's Hanukkah gift from eBay: An almost complete set of Vintage Star Wars figures, and two cases (in the shapes of Darth Vader and C3PO) to store them. It took me three months of bidding, often one figure at a time. It was my attempt to redeem myself for having thrown out all his original figures when he was a kid. When he opened his gift last week, his eyes popped open. "I don't believe you did this! Oh Mom! You're forgiven!"

There was no need to ask if he liked them. He immediately put R2D2 upside down in the bowl of clementines on the table and had Luke and Yoda trying to raise him with the force. "Luke isn't good enough yet," my son said to me. "I think R2 may be stuck here for a while until Luke can harness his power." Unh hunh.

Through eBay bidding, I've gotten my sneakers (Nike, $41.00), my speakers (KLH, $40.00), Mexican coconut masks ($12 each, normally $18-30 in stores), Mexican Christmas tree ornaments ($1.80 each, sold in Katonah for $18.00 each), vegetable crate labels, Treacy's "Old Maid" cards, and the Star Wars stuff (which cost a lot more than my sneakers....).

I've sold a Palm Pilot, a cellular phone, Fiestaware, and Star Wars figures. I'm told that the most popular-selling item on eBay is used underwear. Visit the site if you don't believe me. The ones that fetch the most money are the ones worn for the most days without being washed. It's reassuring to know that if I am ever low on cash, I can sell my dirty laundry.

    I still I haven't found Pullman Porter, although I look every few weeks. It's not like I'm obsessed with it. Anyway, gotta go now. I have to see if I am the high bidder on the Ewok Village and the auction closes in 2 hours.

The Summer of Our Discontent

The summer of 2000 was hell for gardeners and nature lovers. Bugs. Torrential rain. Mold. Slugs. It was the first year that I was officially a gardener by hobby. And I would have considered myself an utter failure had I not consulted more experienced gardening friends who were having the same crummy luck I was. Between the flora, the fauna and merry weather (yes, you detect a chord of sarcasm), growing anything was a challenge.

The year before I'd bought a house that came with a beautiful perennial garden. I saw the blooms when I bid on the house, but when I moved in the late fall, my garden was only a hope. Full of promise. Also full of gross disgusting things that I had no names for until the next spring and summer. Now I know what a grub is, what moles do, how much slugs eat, what a beetle carapace is, what a surprise snowfall does to magnolia blossoms, that ladybugs don't always stick around to eat your aphids, how noisy cardinals really are, why squirrels are not so cute, and that those damn deer will eat anything.

I should say right up front, in case you are thinking of taking up gardening, that there really is no such thing as hobby gardening. Gardening consumes you, the same way slugs get to your leaves. You stumble across a plant you like the look of, be it in a gardening catalogue or at the nursery where you go to buy deer repellant, and suddenly you want it. You'll find room for it. This is how I ended up not only with a perennial garden, but with an herb garden, an annual garden, a shade garden and rock gardens. Oh, and also rose bushes of different varieties (you can't *just* have climbers, you need ground cover too, like Fairy Roses, to protect the roots of the clematis). This is why I used to stay up until late night in the early spring, drinking scotch and reading gardening books the way a teenage boy reads a Victoria's Secret catalogue. Which is to say having active fantasies, only mine were about deer-resistant shade plants or moonlight gardens, all white, that glow at night.

Once I'd gotten the gardens in and was getting in the groove with Mother Nature, with things popping up everywhere in all kinds of colors, it rained. And rained. And rained some more. All my plants got soggy and moldy. I couldn't go out to weed. I decided to turn my attention elsewhere, and realized one bird feeder was not enough. The squirrels agreed, because they were emptying the feeder every day of nuts and seeds. I figured if I got a finch feeder, a suet feeder, a hummingbird feeder, and a squirrel feeder—a squirrel-sized wooden table with two chairs and a place to attach a corn cob—the bird variety would increase and the squirrels would find someplace else to eat. I was wrong. The squirrels not only ate the corn, they chewed holes in all the other feeders and left the birds to fend for themselves.

Of course we have a wild bird store in my town (and the more I think about it, the sillier it seems), so I took the ravaged feeders in to ask what to do next, how to keep the squirrels away. The saleswoman looked at me and asked, "Did a bear get these?" Just so you know exactly what kind of squirrels I'm talking about here. She showed me different squirrel-proof feeders, options that were dizzying. One that gives shocks, one that slides closed over the holes when they hang on the mesh, one that slams shut when they sit their fat butts on the perches.

I am of the "zap the suckers" persuasion, so I was very very tempted to get the battery-charged feeder that jolts them if they contact two metal parts at once (like the platform and a perch). Early that summer I watched with great glee as a friend's squirrels went zinging off his feeder, yelping, each time they tried to get to the seeds. His resident raccoon couldn't get into or onto it either, but that was fine by the raccoon because he busied himself in my friend's garbage cans. But at the wild bird store, my friend Scott convinced me to use a kinder, gentler approach, like the slamming perches model, which I bought. (Scott, who is obviously not of the zapping persuasion, is still using a super-soaker squirt gun loaded with Tabasco and water to greet his marauding squirrels. I predict this will not last.)

So far, I am at an uneasy peace with my squirrels. Not so my friend Kathy, who has vicious kung-fu squirrels who sit in her hickory trees and lie in wait for anyone who approaches her front door. Then they clock you. Pelt. Hammer. It sounds like out-of-synch drumming, which amuses her ten-year old daughter Jessie no end but has actually left bruises on Kathy. Her patio gets six inches deep in nuts in the fall, no joke. The squirrels aren't really eating them or storing them, they take one bite and pitch. Bastids.

And speaking of bastids, we come to the subject of deer. I am naïvely determined to maintain lush gardens. I am certain that if I use Bobbex or Milorganite or Coast of Maine (all of which smell like a mix of very badly soiled underwear and dead fish) on or around my plants, the deer will be repelled. I swear to apply it every week or after every rain, whichever comes first. Shoot, the smell sure keeps *me* out of the garden. I can barely eat on my back patio without gagging. But does the smell stop the deer? Hell no.

Every morning I'd go outside and find something new decimated. Crisp stalks left, but no leaves, no flowers. "Dose bastids!" I'd yell. They worked their way from the hosta (which everyone knows they love) to the hydrangeas to the roses to…well, they ate everything, eventually.

"Dose bastids!" I'd hear out of the phone when Kathy made her daily call to me. "Last night they got the geraniums. They're supposed to hate geraniums."

"Oh, they got mine last week. It was the hollyhocks last night, and the 'I-dunno-what-you-call-em-pink things' that grow by the shady side of my house." Spoken like a true gardening novice.

"But I had a deal with them!" said Kathy earnestly. "I let that doe come up my hill and give BIRTH in front of me, that little baby sounding like a creaky door and nursing for the first time. I have photos! Now they hide in the bushes during the day and just watch me when I'm outside, I know they're there. I can see their ears. When I look away, they eat stuff. DURING THE DAY! They're supposed to be nocturnal. Bastids!"

Summer ended, the nights got cool, and what was left of my garden began to wither on its own. I had given up, for that year. Kathy had too. I imagined Scott would soon, but he was newer than I to gardening and still dewy-eyed. He thought his gardenia bush would survive a winter outside and I didn't have the heart to tell him it wouldn't. He'd learn the same way all of us newbie gardeners did, by our mistakes.

With all the trouble it takes to grow a garden and feed the wildlife, why do we bother? Because the smell of bee balm and hyssop and viburnum and lavender is amazing. Because seeing a metallic green hummingbird sip from my feeder is magical. Because cardinals are exquisite, and no matter what I say, I'm a sap for nature. So I prepare for the next year's garden. I order the daylilies (and put up a fence around where they're going to go). When the leaves are brown, I sprinkle milky spore powder, which prevents grubs, although it takes two years to work. I buy more Bobbex (which I think oughta be called Bobbit and have the ability to neuter deer instantly) and use it every day. Maybe I'll even go the unnatural route of using slug bait rather than beer. Kathy assures me they die happy from beer, like I care how a slug dies.

I wonder if I ought to be more sensitive about taking a life. What right do I have, disturbance in the force and all that. Scott's got a friend who felt so guilty killing a snake that he thought maybe he should eat it to compensate. Well, I wouldn't go that far. But I sure do like venison pepperoni. Maybe, to be a happy gardener, I should become close friends with a hunter.

Decorating with "Wrong Shui"

I know just enough about feng shui to be dangerous. Pronounced "fong shway" by most people in the know, and "feng *shoo*-ey"in Vancouver, which has the largest Chinese population outside of China, it is the theory of harmonious interior decorating using birth years, signs, colors and other auspicious symbols to create wealth, tranquility, and pretty much anything else you would want in your house and life.

The problem with it is that it is confusing. Mirrors must be angled just so, and be eight-sided if possible. The living room must be deep blue or green, the room of family harmony red or orange (or was that the bedroom?), the foot of your bed can't be facing the door of your bedroom, because that's how you're carried out when you're dead. You should not be able to see into any mirror when you are in bed (sorry, all you bachelors with mirrors on the ceiling) because your soul will come out of your body when you sleep and scare itself. You can't have anything under your bed (do my cats count, as long as they are just wrestling and not actually staying there?) or a messy closet—the sign of a cluttered life, you can't have fire next to water, and your toilet can't be at the end of a hall or else it is symbolic of throwing money away, as in "down the toilet." Your toilet lid can't be left open either (again because of losing money, but in my case it's because my cats would swim in the toilet), you shouldn't live in an L-shaped house, you should never live in house number 4 on a street, very unlucky.

Lots of people take feng shui very seriously. In fact, in Vancouver where my friend is an architect, houses often don't receive their Certificates of Occupancy until a feng shui maven comes and pronounces the place to be officially harmonious. This costs about $8,000 and often consists of not much more than a tug on the chin, a thoughtful gaze, and a signature, which is why my architect friend thinks feng shui is a load of hooey. And this guy is pretty open-minded about a lot of things, like psychics and past-life experiences. But not about feng shui.

Stacy and Kathy, on the other hand, my two good friends, swear by it.

"You're NOT putting that candle on the counter next to the cat's water, are you?" asks Kathy.

"I'm not?" I ask. "Why, 'cuz it'll burn the cat's tail?"

"No! Bad feng shui! Very bad."

"But why?"

"I don't know. Just no fire and water together."

Stacy subscribes to some feng shui society newsletter, which I assume features a room of the month and tells her the most auspicious place for, say, the new cappuccino maker or the most propitious shade of green (or was that gray?) bedroom paint. She's warned several people when they are about to commit egregious "wrong shui." (I'd like to say I invented that brilliant term, but I once saw a book with that title. And I thought, "Aha! That's for me!") I also know she has failed to tell people who she doesn't like that they are committing wrong shui. It's kind of her karmic revenge.

But there are remedies for wrong shui. In my case, I was told to add lots of green plants (only live ones, please) to my office because there was something wrong with the position of my desk and the room was too small to have the desk anywhere else. And Kathy, who used to live in Germany at #4 Degerstrasse, in an L-shaped house—a double wrong shui whammy—was told by a feng shui practitioner to paint the number on her house purple and all would be well. Except with the neighbors, who wondered what was wrong with her. Here in New York, her house is also L-shaped, but to remedy it you can plant a bush or bushes outside the house to complete the shape of a square. So she planted rhododendrons, and the deer ate them.

We're looking up the feng shui remedy for repelling unwanted garden pests (painting the bushes purple?), and another to rid the kitchen pantry of moths. Kathy swore there were moth traps in the "Bug and Auto" aisle of the supermarket, and indeed there is such an aisle, but no moth traps.

I'm not really going to let wrong shui get to me. I do the best I can: I keep the toilet lid closed, there are no mirrors opposite my bed, my feet point away from the door when I sleep. Is it so terrible that my slippers are under my bed, or that there are silk flowers in a vase on my dresser? I think not. And you know what? I'm never gonna stop taking baths by candlelight. What's the worst that could happen? I bet Stacy could tell me, but I'd rather not know.

This Dog's Life

When I was very young, and naughty, which was often, my mother would always shout in exasperation, "I hope when you are grown-up and have kids of your own, they are exactly like you!" Well, this didn't happen, exactly. If you ask me, my children are perfect. They are both in college, have not run afoul of the law, and never did anything as imaginatively naughty as I did.

Louis, my empty-nest dog, is another story. A PBGV (short for Petit Basset Griffon Vendeen), he has a reputation all his own. I adopted him four years ago because he had bitten a small child (it turns out the child was trying to remove Louis's tonsils, but I didn't find that out until later) and the breeder told me he needed a home with no kids. So he came to live with me, and within a week was growling at anyone who came near his food or toys, and wouldn't let me brush him without a fight. I started calling him Cujo. I was afraid of him. I called the breeder, and she said, "Clearly he's a problem dog. Take him to the vet and give him the blue juice."

He may have been a discipline problem, but no way was I putting him down. This, I imagined, was my punishment for never making it to Santa's "Nice" list, for driving my own mother crazy. So I was committed to becoming the Alpha Dog in my house (some people would say that's not such a stretch) and getting him to chill out. It took him months to calm down and become a submissive sweetheart who loves cuddles and kisses. But he has never abandoned his genius to wreak mischief.

Louis is mostly a thief. It didn't take him long to figure out the dog door, and then how to raid the laundry basket and find brassieres. He takes them outside with him, and runs back and forth on the lawn with lacy banners streaming from his mouth. Sometimes I catch him in the act and wrestle him, but usually I come home to find my lawn looking like the dressing room of Victoria's Secret.

Besides undergarments, he steals food, or tries to. He stole a pumpkin off my front porch and rolled it down the stairs, down the driveway and into the road. The only reason he didn't eat it was because he couldn't wrap his mouth around it. He figured out how to pull open every cabinet in my kitchen, and has helped himself to cat food, dog treats, protein shakes, paper towels, and even sponges. So I installed child locks. In retaliation, he has learned how to take a hit, run through his invisible fence and go beg from the neighbors, who melt at the sight of his lovable, hairy face.

I get regular phone calls letting me know Louis has arrived at someone's house. My friend Ellen has dubbed him Houdini because he breaks in (never out—the treats are too plentiful; in his next life Ellen's husband wants to come back as a dog, Ellen's dog). Louis wriggles under the fence and walks into her house through her dog door, usually as she is having her morning coffee and I am just starting to wonder where the heck Louis has got to. If she's not home, and he can't score a treat, he leaves his calling card: He takes the toilet plunger out of her bathroom and leaves it in the bedroom, to register his vote of displeasure.

Louis also sings on command. Depressed friends call me up and say, "Put Louis on the phone." So I do, and sing the first few bars of "Oklahoma" or "Happy Birthday" and he begins a yodel that could melt earwax. I hear loud laughter coming out of the earpiece, then I hear, "Thank you," and they hang up.

I've thought of curbing Louis's exuberantly devilish behavior. I've considered boosting the voltage on his receiver collar, and was told there is a special one for "stubborn" dogs. It's triple strength. He already yelps as he bolts across the invisible line, I can just imagine what'll happen if I put the equivalent of a missile launcher around his neck. I don't have the heart to do it. He's just too adorable.

Louis is my best friend. He loves me unconditionally. He makes me laugh. He is the first face I see every morning, and it is always happy. But there's no doubt that he is fulfilling my mother's wish. He is as naughty as they come. Santa's gonna leave Louis a lump of coal in his stocking for sure. Knowing Louis, he'll eat it.

Health and Beauty Tips from Gals on the Go

It's a little-known fact that most of us women get a lot of our personal grooming done in our cars. Not when we're driving—that'd be dangerous, and wouldn't allow us to focus on the beauty task at hand. But while parked and waiting for our kids (to finish school, tutoring, sports, music lessons…), or while stopped in heavy traffic or at a light, we can accomplish a lot.

I thought I was the only woman who kept tweezers, hangnails clippers, emery boards, hand cream and a small scissors in my car's center armrest. Not so. Years ago my friend Pattie admitted that facial hair removal was the perfect car activity because the daylight makes the new growth so easy to see. And in case we miss any strays, our children are all too willing to point out those "rogue hairs" that sprout in the most unwelcome places on our middle-aged visages. So far, I've got four chin "rogues" and the count is on.

Other friends apply makeup (just a lipstick freshening, or undereye concealer) or file their nails. One has mastered hair drying on her way to work: Heat set on high, bi-level. (If you dry your hair with the open window method you get that undesired one-sided look.) Another friend turns her car into a dry sauna on the ride home, then showers off all the toxins and drinks lots of water. Her skin looks great.

Traffic lights are perfect places for us moms to practice Kegels, those lovely little exercises we learned when we were pregnant to keep our bladders from misbehaving. We forget to do them until we sneeze and have an "uh-oh" moment. And then we recommit ourselves to doing them regularly, using some familiar reminder. There's more women out there than you can imagine who see a red octagonal sign and read "SQUEEZE" instead of "STOP."

And the scissors? Well, I have a confession. I'm one of those women who cannot keep her hands off her hair. I trim my curls the nanosecond they inch down below the curve of my ear. Sometimes this happens when I am on the road. I have to pull over. Emergency haircutting is necessary. I figure k.d. lang used to cut her own hair. And curls are very forgiving, I think.

My hair god, Mauro, chastises me, then sighs in resignation as he evens out my sideburns. "You know, *negrita*," he says in his Brazilian accent, "you should not own a scissors. You'll give me a bad name. People will think I did this." But I can't help myself. I may need to start a Haircutter's Anonymous chapter in my neighborhood. I'm not the only one who trims her own hair, you know.

If more men took to grooming themselves in their cars, they'd be much healthier. Look how angry men seem to get when they're stuck in traffic. Instead of feeling powerless and letting their blood pressure skyrocket, putting them at increased risk for heart attacks and strokes, they could get out the tweezers and work on a little personal spruce up. For starters, what about those pesky little ear hairs?

I'll Have the Cyanide, Hold the Mayo

We boomers have been called the sandwich generation, and not because we eat hoagies, wedges, grinders, subs or whatever you call them in your neck of the woods. It's because while we are taking care of our kids, we are also taking care of our aging parents.

It happened to me when I was fairly young—in my thirties—because I had an "older" father. He was 52 when I was born, and I lived with the embarrassment of having an old fart for a dad when I was a teenager. By the time my kids were 7 and 4 years old, I was getting calls from California that my father was doing things like urinating publicly into the fountain in front of Bank of America (can you think of a better place?), and talking back to the screen when he was at the movies. I had to act.

Even though I was a full-time mom, I got my demented father into a nursing home 3,000 miles away, and somehow finished graduate school. Those months are a blur, but *Sesame Street* figures prominently in my memory. I played the same 6-hour video over and over for the kids so I could make the necessary phone calls to Social Security, Motion Picture Welfare Fund, social workers, doctors and other players overseeing my father's care, and write my thesis in relative peace. And then, after all that, my father died, which, in a way, was a blessing.

Now the rest of my friends are suffering through their own versions of this sandwich thing, and I don't envy them. One friend called me from Louisiana—a friend who not only has kids but grandkids too—half out of her mind, to tell me her aging mother had called her and told her everything was going fine with her here in Westchester, that the government was giving out cyanide pills in case our local nuclear plant, Indian Point, blew up.

"Cyanide!?!" she yells, trying to stay calm. "Why is Mother going to take cyanide?"

I tell her it's potassium iodide, for radiation poisoning. Like yeah, that'll help when we are incinerated to kingdom come. But our thyroid glands will be chock full of potassium iodide so we won't get irradiated.

"Oh," she says, feigning an attempt at relief but probably more alarmed than before she called.

Another friend in Ohio writes me daily emails about her brittle-boned mother who broke her leg walking her two dogs, one of whom is a Great Dane. Why an eighty-plus year-old woman walks not one but two dogs, and why she thinks a boisterous Great Dane is an age-appropriate pet, defies logic. Then again, Talia's mom is not logical. And now that she is in a cast, she is kvetching to everyone about the poor care she got from the doctors and nurses in the hospital, the short-term nursing home, at her own house with the home health aide, and from her daughter who has, in her eyes, abandoned her. In fact, the reason Talia has trouble visiting her mother every day is that she is too busy caring for her mother's dogs, her own dogs, her 13-year-old son, and teaching at a university. And feeling guilty. You'd think she was Jewish, but noooooooooo, she's Catholic. It's been pointed out that Jews only know how to use guilt like a seasoning, but Catholics use it as a main ingredient. Just ask Talia. Her mother is complaining that her leg tingles. The *other* leg, not the broken one.

Then there's Reagan, waiting on the East coast by her mother's side for the results of her mom's brain and bone scans to see if there has been any lung cancer metastasis. Reagan's hubby is at home on the Left Coast with their 6 year old, and hubby calls repeatedly to say he cannot work AND take care of a child too. Reagan is considering alcoholism as a treatment for her own angst, except that it runs in the family and she's already tweaked about her increased risk of cancer.

Ellen's got one kid in college, one in high school, and a father-in-law down in Florida who can't keep track of the medications prescribed by about six different specialists who clearly don't talk to each other. This has resulted in several hospitalizations, and Ellen's near apoplexy.

"Didn't they tell you these pills interact with each other?" Ellen asks.

"What's interact?" asks her father-in-law. "All I know, the doctor says I should take them."

"Which doctor?"

"You think I remember?"

Petra's son is unemployed and broke, and Petra's 90-year old dad has leukemia. She's being tugged from two different directions. Petra's mom believes she has the solution for coping well with her husband's illness—she's announced that she is moving to a little house in the hills to live alone, and not trouble anyone. She says she'll take care of herself, if you don't mind. This presents just a weensy problem, because since last year she is legally blind from pressure on her optic nerve, and is having reactions to nearly every medication she takes. But she doesn't want to bother her doctors by complaining; that would just be too forward and not Southern-genteel. She is, after all, a lady. Okay, a crazy lady.

What worries me is that sooner than we think, our children will be the sandwich generation. And I bet if we become anything like our parents, the kids are seriously going to think about playing it fast and loose with us and the cyanide. Who could blame them?

Unorthodox Exes

I went to the best party the other day. I swing-danced with my 18 month-old twin godbabies (or *"ahijados,"* as we call them in Spanish), ate home-made tamales, *bacalao a la Vizcaina, picadillo,* chicken in *mole* sauce, eggrolls (the babies' mom, Maribel, is Peruvian and Chinese), sang the tenor harmonies with a roomful of singers and musicians, ate cake and laughed.

The occasion was my college roommate Stacy's 50th birthday, and what's astonishing is that the party was hosted by her ex-husband, José, and his second wife (the father and mother of the twins). What's also unusual is that my roommate and I are both godmothers of the babies, and we're both called Tia Madrina (which means "Aunt Godmother"—I know this makes no sense). I attended their births, Stacy helped Maribel through the twins' infancies, including driving her to the doctor when she had a breast infection and calling me to help argue with the doctor because Stacy and I thought Maribel was getting bad advice.

And that's not all. My roommate has a new man in her life, and her ex got them together. As her ex walked me to my car after the party, he rubbed his hands together with glee. "Aren't they cute?" he chortled, speaking of his former wife and her beau. "They were holding hands all night, like teenagers!"

Not all exes get exed out of the picture once a marriage ends. Mine comes over on a regular basis, still balances my checkbook, brings me matzoh ball soup when I am sick, and took me out to dinner on my birthday. When it comes to our kids, he and I still function pretty much as a unit and have even traveled together to visit our kids at college. I'm not sure how this happened, that we remain in contact, or why other couples end up avoiding each other or dissing each other. It seems easier to be friends than to be adversaries, less emotional energy gets wasted.

But neither my roommate nor I would ever want to be married to these men again. In fact when we are in lousy moods, we rush to phone each other to be reminded of our respective ex-husband's foibles and transgressions. We know each other's dirty laundry lists as well as we do the other things from our past as party girls, and we go down those lists with evil gusto.

When I am in a slump, Stacy seems to remember more about my marital problems than I do, and vice versa. I recall only good times and get weepy, she dishes. It's always sobering to hear the lowdown again, and comforting too, because without fail we ultimately decide we are happy just as we are. We agree that solitude is not the same as loneliness, that we enjoy having our beds to ourselves and having the freedom to choose if and when to have overnight guests.

Our marital histories are intertwined. My son was 8 months old when Stacy got married and can be heard crying in the background on her wedding tape. I held her daughter, now 18, in my arms, when she was just days old. We have photos of her son and my daughter inspecting the newest lambs (oddly enough, there were twins) born on the farm where Stacy used to live with her husband, and where he now lives with Maribel.

As I walked to the farmhouse door for the party, slogging though the mud that blankets the farm every spring, I was filled with memories and I almost cried. By the end of the evening, though, I'd had a reality check. My goddaughter had given me a fat lip with her hiking boot, my godson had drooled lemon cookie spots all over my black dress, Maribel told me that she and José had been fighting all morning, and Stacy's son, now 20, informed me that he keeps his feather boas fluffy by storing them in the freezer. And I remembered that instead of a party, my ex gave me "re-gifted," stale candy for my birthday.

Still, it's a delight to have reconfigured our relationships with our former husbands so that we can still laugh. Granted, sometimes we're laughing at them, like when Stacy's ex had to retrieve 10 pounds of potatoes that the twins dropped into the basement through a hole in the floor, or when my ex ended up in the emergency room three times in two weeks but kept insisting he was fine. Bottom line, we still like our exes. In fact, I just asked mine this morning if he knew a nice man he could introduce me to.

Meet and Delete

The only good thing I can say about cyber-dating is that I met Jamie, one of my best women friends, through a personal ad. She saw an ad I had online when she was placing one herself and trying to get ideas, and wrote me to say it was the most articulate, funny, forthright personal she had ever read and wished me luck.

Luck, and plenty of it, is what we both have needed. Jamie's a university professor in a Northeastern city, and we have stayed in constant touch over the last six months, bellyaching over what she calls cretins and doofuses, and sharing the emails our prospective suitors have sent us (they should only know). Between us we have power-dated enough men (and a few women) to make a sorority happy.

Through my old internet ad I've dated people with legendary bad breath (I modified the ad to say "someone who flosses daily," since there seem to be so many people to whom this form of hygiene is foreign); someone who lied about his disability and kept falling down my front steps every time we went out (no I am NOT making fun of the disabled, I've got a disability myself, so hold yer damn letters to the editor; and no, I don't know why we had more than one date, okay?); people who turned out to be smokers when their ads said definitely not; and one polyamorous widower whose wife was barely cold before he started convincing his online prospects that monogamy is for wussies who don't truly honor their partner's freedom. Un hunh.

Jamie, a nice widow in her 40's, is just as discriminating as I am. Although we both agreed that college degrees are important, we also reminded ourselves that school is a relatively new invention in the history of humankind, and folks like Mark Twain got along just fine without formal schooling. So we looked for partners whose traits included humor, tenderness, and biting intelligence. She added lack of flatulence to her list (but was too kind to put it in her personal ad) after an impeccably credentialed gent flew all the way from the Left coast to meet her and got stuck in her son's bathroom with a gas attack. She said she was trying not to hear the dreadful body noises, but, says she, even *one* of them, like a dandruff flake, is just too much for a first date.

We've argued over when it's okay to finally sleep with someone if the chemistry is there—do we follow The Rules, that very stupid book by two women (now both divorced) that advises women to never initiate a relationship, never call a man back, never sleep with him until you have an engagement ring? What if we don't want to get married again? There are other informal rules on the subject, and finally we threw them all out and decided to follow our mature hearts. Keep some mystery yes, but beguile, ensnare, dare I say *tease*? Never.

The problem with email courtship is that it's a lot like Victorian letter writing, so full of mush and romance and idealization that it's hard not to be disappointed when you finally meet. (And who Jamie has met, of course, are cretins and doofuses, plus one "true repulsivo" with a mean scar on his face and a penchant for Dr. Laura.) So instead of the protracted electronic courtship, we decided it was best to "meet and delete," not keep writing and fantasizing.

That phase is nearing its end, too, I think. Jamie is now dating someone from her church and someone from her History department. Me, I'm hooked up with a friend's brother, someone who knew my ex-husband in high school (and I'll have you know, even though I threw up on our fourth date, he hasn't dumped me, which Jamie would surely have done if I were dating her).

Not that there aren't stellar Internet love stories. I personally know of two that would make you weep. But Jamie and me? We're pulling our ads and it looks like we're gonna stick with local yokels.

Cronehood's Only Just Begun

I heard recently that over 40 million women are about to begin menopause. I hope it's not all on the same day.

The esteemed doctor who made this pronouncement, Christiane Northrup, MD, is a member of my baby-boomer generation. She says that menopause (or as my friend Kathy and I call it, "mental pause") can begin in the mid-forties to mid-fifties and that the symptoms last up to 10 years. That it's kinda like PMS, only all the time. Great, just great.

If you're at all faint-hearted, I recommend you stop reading now. But for those of you who want to be well informed—because you yourself are a perimenopausal woman, friends with one, married to one, or just play one on TV—read on.

Grrrls, here's what we can expect: Sleeplessness, waking early, irritability, night sweats, irregular periods, memory loss, hot flashes, and loss of libido. Some women get some, or all, or none of the above. Some women just stop having periods, and finally realize they are now postmenopausal. Then again, maybe they have that memory loss thing happening and don't remember that their periods are irregular. I mean, who can keep track, what with counting hot flashes and changing the sweaty sheets.

There are some less common symptoms as well, like heart palpitations, growth of chin hairs, graying pubic hair, mysterious bruises, anxiety, migraines, low back pain, development of new allergies, indigestion, depression, "crawly skin" (known as formication, not to be confused with fornication), and my personal favorite, waking up with sore heels.

Who doesn't have some of these symptoms? (If you're a man, of course, you disregard the growth of chin hairs.) So the next step is figuring out whether it's the beginning of menopause or whether you're dying of some strange disease, a conclusion I leap to almost immediately.

Obviously, the first thing to do is check in with your doctor. You'll probably be told that symptoms that are cyclical are good, because it means they are caused by fluctuations in hormones. And to hang in there, if you can, until your symptoms are unbearable, or until your significant other moves out, whichever comes first.

Then comes the question, hormone replacement therapy (HRT) or not? The newest studies indicate that HRT does not prevent heart disease in women and actually doubles the risk of ovarian cancer. So what are we supposed to do? Suffer? I don't think so.

I've heard arguments that taking hormones is unnatural, and anyway what did women in the olden days do? I'll tell you what they did: They died young. They maybe never got this far. They had babies at 16, and croaked in their thirties and forties.

We boomers are damn healthy, and are living a long time. Long enough to become science experiments for future generations to know that if you are on HRT from your fifties to your eighties, it's just fine. Or maybe not fine.

As for me, I really don't want to take hormones if I can avoid it. I am sure at some point, I will beg for them. Meanwhile, I want to live through peri- and post-menopause, and everything in between, for as long as I can stand it. I want to become, in the words of Germaine Greer, a crone. A wisewoman. A *femme sage*. One of those types who's respected because she's an elder and has a few gray pubic hairs and no one's gonna say "boo" to.

Soon there'll be lots of us. Dr. Northrup says that we are going to be the most powerful economic and social force ever in history. No kidding. Forty million women who feel like they are having PMS all the time? There will be roving hordes of us, having our say, getting our way. But of course, we'll have to rove in the afternoons, because in the mornings, our heels will be sore.

Clothing Optional

I'm cranky. We've had three snowstorms since the New Year, my front porch could be backup for the local skating rink, I've cut my hands removing icicles, and I'm cold all the time. I don't like cold. Neither does the man who styles my curls, my Brazilian hair god Mauro, who complains that he's so cold his nipple rings keep popping out.

What I miss right now is the nude beach at Robert Moses State Park. Technically, it's not a nude beach. As you trek in, heading toward the Fire Island lighthouse, you come to a sign that says, "You are entering a clothing optional area." Which means, you wanna wear a bathing suit? Fine, be that way. But you don't have to if you don't want to.

Most people who go there choose not to wear clothes. I'm one of them. And it's not because I'm an exhibitionist like Mauro is. It's because I can relax and not worry about what people think I look like in a bathing suit.

If you know about women, you know that, for any of us, being seen in a bathing suit is a traumatic event. I've never met a woman yet who didn't dislike something about how her body looks in Lycra. And when all of us are in swimsuits together, well, it's kind of like we are in some sort of undeclared beauty pageant. Comparisons are inevitably made.

The stress of worrying if your abs are tight enough or does your butt look too cottage-cheesy or should you have gone for a maillot instead of a thong....well, it's too much for me to deal with. I go to the beach because I like the sound and feel of the water, and I love the relaxing warmth of the sun. I can't relax if I feel I am being judged.

For some reason, when you're at a nude beach, the judging stops. Hey, we're all naked there. Vulnerable. And therefore somehow safer with each other. It's quite humbling.

I've been going to nude beaches since I was sixteen and realized I was never going to have the body of a model. I was even arrested once, but not for indecent exposure. It's because I was lying on someone's Masters thesis on soil erosion on a private beach in Santa Barbara. I believe the stuff I crushed was called ice plant. Anyway, the cop let me go if I promised never to trespass again. But he was grinning when he said it. I've frolicked naked on Venice Beach in the days when hippies were there, not gangs. I've trekked into canyons in Mexico to go naked in hot springs rather than be viewed on the beach in Puerto Vallarta. I will go to great lengths not to have to wear a bathing suit.

Sure, there are voyeurs at these places. The first time I went to Robert Moses State Beach, with my girlfriend Zee, we stripped, lay down on our towels and began to talk. After about a half an hour, two naked women came up to us and said, "Uh ladies, you may want to move, or put up a screen. That guy on the beach below you? He's a real perv. He probably knows by now whether you've had tonsillectomies."

The two, both public school teachers, sat down on our towels and taught us The Nude Girls Beach Rules: Avoid that guy who wears his tee shirt wrapped around his head and squats in front of you to talk, his parts dangling in the breeze. Avoid the "Winnie the Poohs," men who wear only shirts over their fat bellies, just like a certain fictional bear. Ignore the guys who ask you to put sunblock on their backs. Never, ever look into the eyes of those guys who are lying flat on their stomachs with their hands underneath them—you know what they're doing, and they don't need encouragement. Put up a screen *below* where you're lying. And don't forget to put sunblock on yourself in places you normally wouldn't think to.

We'd already broken all the rules our first time out. It was a truly painful lesson. But we learned fast, and were never bothered, or sunburned, again. We became friends with the crowd of regulars, all professionals with real jobs, and shared food and good laughs. We taught The Rules to nekkid newbies. We'd howl at the teenage boys who used to sneak down the beach past the "Clothing Optional" sign to get a thrill, only to embarrass themselves by being completely out of control of their bodies' reactions to naked women. Our teacher friends would holler at them, "What would your mothers say, you Peeping Toms! Either take your shorts off or get out of here! And get those peckers down!"

Our long walks down the beach all together in the altogether, hunting for beach glass (red is the hardest to come by, then blue—serious trading goes on during sunny weekends), took us to the Fire Island Light beach, where the nudity, mostly male, gets downright competitive. I could picture Mauro here in his glory, his jewelry sparkling, his toned body on display. This is a man with a nude photo of himself on the Internet. He even works out in the buff at his gym. He lives to rip his clothes off. On New Year's Eve, partygoers make bets on how long his clothes would stay on. (Last year, whoever bet on three minutes past midnight was the winner.)

This flamboyant kind of nudity is not my idea of a good time. I take my clothes off to hide, to blend in with nature. When Mauro's naked, it's a personal *Rio Carnavale*. But we do agree on one thing: Beach weather can't come soon enough.

Godiva's Got Nothing on Me

I can now die a happy woman. Some people dream of winning a Grammy, or the Nobel Peace Prize, or the Pulitzer Prize. Julia may finally have her Oscar, and I know people who have won Emmies, Clios, MacArthur "Genius" awards, and Rhodes scholarships. But those honors pale, in my opinion, next to the honor bestowed on me: A chocolate truffle now bears my name.

The "Julietta" was designed by Maarten Steenman, the genius who creates amazing desserts at La Tulipe in Mount Kisco, New York. I was hooked on the place when I sampled the lemon tart two summers ago. Since then, I think I have tasted every cake he makes. My favorite, the "Tulipe Noire" (or Black Tulip), will surely earn him a place in baker's heaven—a chocolate mousse cake laced with flavor of caramelized sugar, like you'd find at the bottom of a flan or on top of a crème brulee. On New Year's Eve, my Boston friends pronounced it the best cake ON EARTH.

I'm not sure when I developed my passion for chocolate. Maybe it began when my Aunt Leah brought me chocolate shaped like matzohs for Passover one year. Or as a result of the chocolate-covered orange peels my mother bought me on special occasions. Perhaps it was when I lived in Europe and tasted my first real chocolate, in the form of chocolate mousse, at Benni's Bar in Ibiza. Or maybe it was because my father always used to say that certain dumb so-and-so's didn't "know shit from chocolate" and I was determined never to be such an ignoramus.

So I learned my chocolates. I know a good milk chocolate from a bittersweet, a mousse from a ganache, how to cook Mexican chicken in *mole* sauce using chocolate, chile, and sesame seeds. I like highbrow and lowbrow chocolates, just so long as they taste good to me. Godiva truffles are yummy, but so are Snickers bars. I don't like all chocolate though; I don't eat white chocolate, Hershey's kisses, chocolate ice cream, or chocolate covered pretzels. Blech.

I crave chocolate, especially when there's a chance I may not be able to get my hands on any. When we had the last Nor'easter, and I knew I was going to be stuck in the house for maybe days, I almost panicked. But my friend Treacy in California, who understands this sort of thing, FedExed me emergency chocolate. My box of See's candies arrived intact during the snowfall, and the pecan caramel clusters, molasses honeycombs and almond toffees soothed me better than any roaring fire could have.

As everyone knows, chocolate contains some feel-good substance that makes your brain behave as if you were in love. After you consume it, you feel buzzed, a little euphoric, and lose the desire to eat, or at least, I do. And dentists say chocolate is preferable to other desserts, as it does not stick to your teeth. So chocolate is an anti-depressant, anti-cavity diet aid—what could be bad?

Over the years, my family and friends realized that to give me a box of Godiva truffles (mandarin orange was my favorite), no matter the occasion, was the best gift ever. I would make the candies last and last, doling out one truffle to myself every two or so days. I'd count them, so I'd know if small children had discovered my hiding places. I'd maybe share.

But obtaining Godiva truffles from a *bona fide* Godiva store is costly and, from where I live, inconvenient. You can buy them prepackaged elsewhere, but then they are not as fresh or as good. They are also sold over the Internet, but the shipping fees are astronomical. I needed a local, top-quality connection for chocolate fixes.

So, on my regular trips to La Tulipe for orange brioches, I always asked why Maarten didn't have any handmade chocolate orange truffles. Okay, Maarten says I bugged him. I like to think of it as cajoling. In any case, I somehow got my wish. Maybe it's because Maarten and his wife had just had a new baby, Lydia, and Maarten was feeling magnanimous. Or maybe because he was thrilled that he had just mastered an incredibly difficult baking feat, making a champagne mousse cake that really, really tasted like champagne.

Whatever his reasons, Maarten caved. I got to go into La Tulipe's kitchen and sample various strengths of orange-flavored ganaches, made with imported pure fruit essences. I got to taste different chocolates and make executive decisions like, "no Grand Marnier."

My friends joined me for the final truffle tasting. (Maarten said we should come early, as it was better to eat chocolate in the morning, as your taste buds are more alive then. My kind of guy.) Eyes bugged, women moaned, and one friend was rendered speechless by the intense deliciousness of the samples. And then I chose the winner.

The "Julietta" is an orange ganache truffle enrobed in dark chocolate with grated, candied orange peel in it. Maarten kindly lied and told the press that he named the truffle after me because Julietta was a beautiful and elegant name, not because I am such a *noodge*.

I imagine people across Westchester, nay, all up and down the East coast, saying, "And pick me up a pound of Julietta truffles please." Farfetched? I don't think so. Maarten's gaining fame far and wide. Last weekend I stayed in Philadelphia, and my innkeepers, when they heard where I was from, asked me, "Isn't that where La Tulipe is? We had the best pear almond tart from there...."

So, I have been immortalized by a confectionery star. I am getting congratulatory phone calls. I am ecstatic, blessed. It's better than if Paul Simon had written a song for me. I'm high on cacao. I keep dipping into my little cellophane bag of "Juliettas" to savor yet another one of my namesakes.

And in case you were wondering: Yes, it is possible to eat too much chocolate.

Big Boy Cars

My best male friend Eric called me recently to tell me he was getting a new car. A Lincoln. My response was polite silence, but in my head, I screamed *A LINCOLN!!!!! Oy! Are you nuts?*

This was Eric, Eric! You have to understand, this is the guy I inhaled with, the guy on whose deck I sunbathed naked, the guy I sat next to at college graduation, our caps barely fitting on our heads because our 'fros were so big. This is the guy who married a woman who is my sister at heart, and we had our babies within weeks of each other, in the same birth center, with midwives. We were even in the room during the births of each other's kids. Until my kids became of age, Eric and his wife were my kids' legal guardians should anything happen to the ex and me, and their daughters are like my very own.

And he's buying a Lincoln? Lincolns are driven by old Jewish men with big bellies, white belts, and wet cigars sticking out of their mouths: My uncles, in other words. Or by black men in color-coordinated outfits, say lavender or lime green, right down to the fishnet undershirt and silk boxers, with pinkie rings that spell their names in 47 diamonds: My friend and black linguistics professor, Sweet Ernie, in other words.

Or perhaps nowadays, Lincolns are driven by men who immigrate to the U.S. and work for car services, men who may have left to escape *fatwas* against folks like Jews, Salman Rushdie, or people who believe in personal freedom. Then they come here and exercise their freedom with wild and crazy abandon on the roadways and scare the bejeepers out of all the folks who obey things like stop signs and red lights. Like the guy who drove me and the kids to the airport in a Lincoln Town car. The driver swerved so much and so hard that the kids both fell off the back seat onto the floor. I was not happy.

"That! That's a Lincoln!" I pointed out to my daughter a few weeks ago when we saw a 1960's Continental on the FDR. "What my Uncle Sol called a Jewboat."

So, I kept my opinions to myself about Eric's new toy, only to find out I didn't have to because his daughters were not going to let him bring it home and had beat me to the diss. Until they saw it, and rode in it. And then I got my chance. And was glad I had said nothing, and thus did not have any words to eat.

Eric's father-in-law lives in Palm Springs and loves to wear shorts. Whenever he goes out to dinner, his wife always says "Honey, time to put on the Big Boy pants." I guess there comes a time in everyone's life when we have to accept that we have to put on the Big Boy pants, that we're grownups, even me, even Eric. We have to face the fact that, for some of us, the only thing we inhale anymore is nasal spray.

I have to admit it: His car is *way* cool. It's black and sexy and has black leather seats. It's by no means a Jewboat, more like a slick little cigarette boat, the kind they rode all the time on Miami Vice, a show Eric used to edit. I like his car for the same reason Eric does. It's a responsible, adult car. And it goes REALLY fast.

Press This!

Today I called my medical group. Ten years ago I would have said, "I called my doctor," but doctors are now private corporations, medical groups, or huge patient mills like the place I called. It's enough to make you sick.

What I hate most are the answering systems these places use. When I called, I heard, "You've reached the Medical Group. If this is an emergency, go to the hospital. If you are a doctor, press 1. If you wish to make an appointment, press 2; to renew a prescription, press 3; if you'd like to speak to a doctor, press 0 for the Operator."

Well of course I wanted to speak to a doctor! That's why I called. And instead I was going to speak to the Operator? And tell her my personal business? I don't think so.

In my frustration, I decided maybe I'd leave this conglomerate and switch to a single doctor in an individual practice. Okay, I admit, I even had a fleeting, wild fantasy about house calls. So I called my HMO (which in my opinion stands for Hand the Money Over) to ask which doctors were participating providers on my plan.

I got a voicemail system. "If you are calling about a claim, press 1; if you'd like a list of providers, press 2; if you are calling about the new prescription plan, press 3; for...." I figured I'd beat the system and press 0 for an Operator.

Says a pre-recorded voice, in a heavy Noo Yawk accent, "You have made an invalid choice. Please try again."

Now I'm ready to throw the phone. I start over and have to listen to the whole menu of options to find out that to speak to a real human, I must press 6.

I am sure there are people whose jobs are to think up voicemail programs that are user-*un*friendly, systems that thwart consumer's attempts to reach customer service (ha!—now there's an oxymoron) and have what is now referred to as an "interactive dialogue." Those diabolical inventors probably even track how many people, like me, actually press the default "0" for an operator instead of waiting the torturous amount of time and proper number of keypad pokes necessary to get to a live individual. And I bet they wring their hands gleefully and cackle at the number of idiots, I mean customers, they outsmart.

All this reminds me of a day many years ago when two psychiatrist friends of mine were joking that soon there would be automated suicide hotlines. "If you are planning to kill yourself, please press 1. If you called this number in error, please hang up now." Once the desperate individual, presumably standing on a ledge with his portable phone (this was before the days when everyone had a cell phone) had pressed 1, he'd hear, "If you plan to slit your wrists, press 1; if you are going to overdose, press 2; if you intend to hang yourself, press 3; if you're a jumper, press 4; if you plan to attach tubing to your exhaust pipe with duct tape and sit in your car in your garage inhaling carbon monoxide until the police find you, press 5."

Sadly, my friends' scenario was not far from the truth. I can't think of an institution today that doesn't have voicemail. I do know of one brokerage firm with a sense of humor. Their phone menu said "...and if you want to hear a duck quack, press 8." And sure enough, if you pressed 8, a duck quacked. It was good for a laugh. But it didn't get me any closer to a human.

If you are as annoyed as I am about this, press 1. If you think this is a more efficient way to run life, press 2. To hear me scream, press this!

You Do the Math

Just last week, I asked my son when he would have free time to do some website design for me. His reply included the hours that he worked his day job (10-6) and the hours he worked his night job (7-1) and the hours he had band practice (weekends, mostly) and the dates he had real, live, paid music gigs, and then he said, "You do the math."

I don't know about you, but those are some terrifying words. My friend Eve says that as far as she is concerned, they are the four scariest words in the English language. I know plenty of bright women, like attorneys and doctors, who say that when it comes to discussing numbers, it's like a steel door shutting in a maximum security prison, a huge clanging boom in their brains that says, "NO MATH BEYOND THIS POINT."

I don't think this is a gender issue. I know lots of other bright women who manage millions of dollars in budgets and stock portfolios for work, for clients, and—for a few lucky ones—themselves. But I have to tell you, I'm in the first group.

It didn't always used to be this way. In high school I got 100 on my algebra final, and 100 on my geometry final. A lot of good that's done me in daily life. Okay, so I use the Pythagorean theorem on occasion, but I wouldn't know a binomial from a bowl of oatmeal. I never made it to trigonometry or calculus, subjects my son reads about—for fun. I did pass statistics, twice, but all I can remember is mean, mode and median. Which is which? Don't ask me.

But I manage to pay my bills and run a household budget. I even got me a brand new mortgage recently. However, it was kind of a foggy experience for me. All I know is that mortgage rates had come down, and it was supposed to be a good idea to refinance. Three other women

112

I knew had just done it, or were about to do it, and they were throwing out interest rates with alacrity. Seven. Seven point two five. Six point eight. Bingo! I had no idea what this meant in terms of actual dollars, but I sort of knew lower was better. Especially because when I locked at 6.8% my friend Kathy said, "I hate you." This, in girlfriend-ese means, "You've done good."

The morning of the signing, I panicked. I called my friend Zee, who knows how to refinance, and I hyperventilated, "I can't do this. I'm not really a grownup. Now everyone will know! How do I know what I'm signing?"

"First of all, breathe," she advised me. "And you can do it. Just go and sign, and sign, and sign. It takes forever, you write your full name about a hundred times, and then you have three days to change your mind about everything."

"An escape clause? Oh thank God."

"Bring your papers over when you're done and I'll look them over."

That evening we had a three-way pow-wow. One post-refinancee, two pre-refinancees.

"You got six point eight? Lucker!" says Linnie.

"Yeah. Kathy said she hates me. That's good right?"

"Definitely," says Zee.

"Wait," says Linnie. "I'm gonna be paying way more than you every month. That's not fair. And I got seven. Why is my payment so much more?"

Much handwringing ensued. Voice messages were left to her mortgage broker, telling him how angry she was, telling him even though it was 11PM there was still an hour for her to rescind her agreement. Of course we couldn't figure out how to do that, but we thought the threats sounded good.

Only problem was Linnie had accidentally been calling some dentist's cell phone. He called her the next morning to say he really wished he could give her a better rate on her mortgage, but he only worked on teeth. Her broker never got her calls, which was just as well, because it turned out she was only paying $50 more a month than I was (the difference was in our school taxes, our smart, financially-savvy friend Zee figured out).

    I'm so excited that now I can say things like "rescission period" and "I locked at" and "points." But I don't know what the hell I'm talking about. All I know is I pay less per month than I used to, I have no more credit card debt, I own my car outright, and my mortgage broker made a wheelbarrow full of money on the deal. But I still can't do the math.

Singin' in the Pain

I don't know about you, but when life just overwhelms me, when I am stricken with such a severe case of anhedonia that I can barely put one foot in front of the other, song lyrics jump into my head.

Linnie calls. Her teenage son has just called her a "fucking bitch." She is nearly in tears. I start singing to her, "Kids! What's the matter with kids today?"

She joins in, we are two Ethel Mermans singing into two telephone mouthpieces, "Why can't they be like we were, perfect in every way? What's the matter with kids tooooooooo-daaaaaaaaay?"

Another girlfriend is going through a divorce (well jeez, come to think of it, I have four girlfriends getting divorced, a scary thought), working out the details of the agreement. As if it is ever truly an agreement, ha! Such arguing you shouldn't know from: He earns more, she earns more, he lets himself in the house without calling first, helps himself to the mustard or whatever, she switches the kid dates on him and it interferes with his time with his girlfriend…oy.

So my friend has to go to court because mediation, in her case, is a joke. We imagine a scene where the judge hears that her soon-to-be-ex cannot afford to pay her alimony because he doesn't earn enough, and the judge asks him, "But you don't actually *work*, do you?" Then the judge, who happens to sing bass, and the bailiff and the court reporter and everyone else jumps up and starts singing doo-wop style, "Doo-doo-doo-doo, doot-de-doot-de-doo-doo….GET A JOB!" We find this deliciously funny.

When I first got divorced, I was miserable. I flung myself around my empty house, weeping, and could hear the swells of violins in my head and a vibrato voice warbling, "Can't live, if livin' is without you, I can't liiiiiive, I can't live anymore...."

I got over this period rather quickly. I found myself bopping around, dustrag in hand, belting, "Got along without before I met you, gonna get along without you now." I cleaned with a fervor, the rhythm of South Pacific's "Gonna wash that man right out of my hair..." pushing me to new heights of household tidiness.

Now I walk around the house singing the tenor part of Haydn's "Lord Nelson" Mass and Vivaldi's Dixit, because that what we Master Singers are singing this fall. Incongruously, I also find myself singing, "Wild things, you make my heart sing!" to my Bengal cats, which just goes to show you the depth of my song-lyric affliction.

But I swear, this really does help in times of trouble (I just heard Art Garfunkel in my head singing, "Like a bridge over troubled water, I will lay me down," which, now that I think about I, makes no sense). I'm not sure why songs help. Or music in general. Maybe it's the universality of it. If words are written, music composed, songs recorded for posterity, they must appeal to us on that level where communication fails us.

A conductor I know (symphony, not choo-choo train) conducted a concert in Brazil the night after the September 11 terrorist attacks here in the U.S. Before the musicians took up their instruments, the man asked the orchestra and the audience to pause for a moment of silence in remembrance of lives lost and dreams shattered. Then he said, "Now, let's show the world what beautiful things the human spirit is capable of."

Not all music exalts the soul. Not mine anyway. Ix-nay on country songs with titles like "I Got Tears in My Ears from Lying on My Back in My Bed Being Blue over You." Ditto for gangsta rap and heavy metal. But I realize it's a question of taste. Maybe you like to meditate to Metallica. As my grandmother would have said, "So nu, do it in good health!"

And what am I singing to myself these days, besides "America the Beautiful?" Well, sometimes I'm hearing Gloria Gaynor's "I Will Survive." Sometimes it's Cat Steven's "Ooh, baby, baby it's a wild world..." or his "Morning has broken, like the first morning..." Ironically, Cat Stevens became a Muslim in 1977, and goes by the name Yusuf Islam, which he adopted because the word Islam comes from the Arabic word for peace, salaam. (In a press release, Yusuf Islam condemned the horrific carnage of September 11, mourned the loss of innocent lives and supported America in its quest for justice.)

But mostly, I've got John Lennon in my head: "Imagine all the people, living life in peace...You may say I'm a dreamer, but I'm not the only one, I hope some day you'll join us, and the world will live as one."

Salon Secrets Revealed!

A lot of people, especially men, must wonder why so many women go to nail salons. I'll tell you: It's the heated vibrating chairs.

That of course is not the only reason salons are so popular. But sitting on a hunka burnin' buzz while someone paints your toenails is definitely a major attraction for most of us. Then there's also the full foot massages, pressure point massages with little wooden sticks, lovely hot honey and salt scrubs on your legs, grapefruit lotion massages on your hands, and shoulder, neck and head massages while your nails dry under the fans.

The conversation and camaraderie are also a lot of fun. If you go with a friend, and are lucky enough to sit next to her, that's one kind of social event. Another is finding yourself between two women, or between mothers and daughters (this is often a mother-daughter activity), who are talking to each other over the heads and hands and feet of others.

I've overheard, "I don't think I'm ever going to finish menopause. At my wake, my friends will be throwing Maxipads into my coffin." And, mother to noodging daughter, "Jesse, if you kick me again, I'll make you bleed." I've heard how marriages have failed and why. And that Girl A's boyfriend cheated with Girl B, but Girl A is still going to the prom with him because she already has the dress and the painted nails. After the prom, Girl A swears that she will arrange that soon-to-be-ex-boyfriend will never be able to bear children.

Nail salons are also places you can take a date, maybe not willingly though. Last weekend at the salon I saw two obviously divorced parents (no married couple would talk to each other so much, blush so much, or look to be in such a perpetual state of public arousal). She was in red snakeskin boots with carefully mussed hair to give it that just-out-of-bed-all-I-could-find-was-this-red-matching-barrette look, and skintight jeans. She kept running her tongue over her red-painted lips, and she was so eager for her date to arrive her eyes were almost bulging. She had her daughters with her, and he showed up with his, and the girls got manicures and pedicures. The divorced mom snapped photos of all and the divorced man looked uncomfortable most of the time, especially when his date said, "Oh look! 'Wicked!' That's the name of the color I wear!" And she put the bottle in front of his face for examination. He feigned interest, another clue he was for *sure* not her husband.

From the warm vibrating chairs, if you can keep your eyes open, you can watch the flow of traffic in and out of the waxing rooms, where hair on various parts of the body (lips, eyebrows, legs, "bikini area," even underarms) gets yanked out. You never hear screaming either. After all, women can bear children, so for us mothers, waxing pales in comparison. I have to admit though: I had natural childbirth, twice, but would happily have an epidural for my next bikini wax.

Except for the occasional man who gets his chest hair waxed (I find that revolting—I like a guy with a furry chest), and maybe the few men who have manicures or pedicures (hold the polish), there's not much testosterone in nail salons. Sometimes there are male manicurists, but most of them seem to be testosterone-challenged. And in my opinion, they do not paint nails as well as women. You end up with polish on your cuticles and skin and have to go home and redo it. Maybe this is because not enough men wear nail polish and know how to do it right. But do we want men to proliferate in these enclaves?

The truth is, a nail salon is a woman's refuge. We get a kick out of polish names like "Vampire State Building," "Plymouth Lox," and "You Cannoli Imagine." Nail salons are the female response to massage parlors, only we don't need no stinkin' rub-and-tug. We're happy with rub-and-paint. And I think we want to keep it that way.

Libby Gets a Nose Job

Last summer my friend's daughter, Libby, broke her nose in the stupidest way imaginable.

Being 19 and impulsive, she kicked off her shoe, a big clunky one, while aiming at her boyfriend's head. Although this in itself is an act of astonishing dumbness, what happened next is even worse. The shoe sailed into the air, and came right back down. On Libby's nose.

"Instant karma," says Libby, for whom the embarrassment should have been enough punishment. But there was pain too. And black eyes. She put ice on her nose and waited for Stacy, her mom and my best friend from college, to take her to the ER.

More explaining was necessary there, as the staff was hard put to believe Libby could have done this to herself and they wanted to call Social Services. But once Libby's nose had officially been pronounced busted, Stacy got the go-ahead to leave the next day on their planned trip to "Califordia," as Libby was now calling it.

I extracted a promise from Stacy that she would call plastic surgeon Jane Petro when she returned. So on January 9th (FIVE months after the incident, I'd like to point out) Libby, Stacy and I had an appointment with the good doctor.

Before we left for Dr. Petro's office, we visited the doc's website to learn all about rhinoplasty, the polite term for nose job. I got sidetracked by the special cases.

"Libby, look! A head in tar! How cool is this? Look at the beautiful reconstructive work."

"Yew!" says the patient-to-be.

"Okay, how about this one? A severed hand! Awesome."

"YEWWWW!" yells Libby. "Show me noses, I want to choose a nose."

So we learned all about the procedure and made printouts to take with us to ask intelligent-sounding questions.

Our attempt to appear smart was doomed when Dr. Petro said to Libby, "You did this to yourSELF? Let me shake your hand."

The nurse popped in a video for us to watch. We're imagining tarred and severed. "Is this gonna be gross?" I ask.

"No, but there is one rule," says the nurse, who is taking us and life entirely too seriously, "you MUST pay attention."

That did it. As the door closed, we began snickering into our cupped hands. "Does this remind you of 5th grade when they showed you the Kotex film?" I ask Stacy. "Uh hunh," she muffles into her palm.

We endured the film, with bad actors telling us that rhinoplasty had come a long way in the last 100 years. "I'm sure!" screeches Libby, as she mimes a doctor punching someone in the nose and yells, "POW! Your nose'll be fine now!"

Stacy and I are our sliding out of our chairs laughing and Libby is pummeling the exam chair with the heels of her boots as Dr. Petro walks back in. Rolling her eyes at us all, she turns to me and asks, "Am I supposed to thank you for this referral?"

I hang my head, but Stacy and Libby are still snorking, even as the doctor turns Libby's face this way and that and we are awed by her skilled, gentle fingers. So I giggle too.

Dr. Petro asks Libby what kind of nose she wants. This leads to a long discussion of options, ending with the solemn promise to Libby that people will ask her, "Did you just get back from a great vacation?" Not, "Isn't that a Petro nose?"

As we ponder nose possibilities, the doctor begins to speak into her little Dictaphone, highlighting the case and ending with something like, "Patient undecided about exactly how she'd like her nose to look, but wants it centered in the middle of her face…" And we're off on another round of snickering. "Is there anyone who ever asks for their nose NOT to be in the middle of their face?" I can barely ask through giggles.

I get that *Un Chien Andalou* stare from the dear doctor, and I shut up. "You know," she tells Libby, "they don't have to be in the room with you. You are the patient."

"No," says Libby, still a kid after all. "I want my mama here. And I want Julietta so mama doesn't yell at me like she always does when I am sick." It's a wonder they didn't try to call Social Services. Again. Libby's surgery is scheduled. She and Stacy will stay at my house the night before, and maybe the day after, and I may even get to go into the OR with Libby before they knock her out. We're all a little scared and a little excited. A new nose! Breathing! But we've learned one thing from this: If the shoe fits, wear it. Don't throw it.

Puttin' on the Kitsch

Let's face it, Jews just don't have enough icons. Gentiles get to wear Easter bonnets, silly headbands with reindeer antlers, Christmas tree sweaters that light up. They have candles of patron saints who'll help save your dog, get you pregnant, and protect your home. They even eat exotic icons like Communion wafers. We have gefilte fish.

Gentiles make festive Jello molds, we mold chopped liver. Gentiles have burning incense, we have burning chicken fat. Gentiles drink martinis, we drink that God-awful kosher sweet wine. They have pigs in blankets, we have pigs in blankets, but ours are Hebrew National, 100% beef. (So should we really be calling them *pigs?*) Jews don't have Lent, but we don't need it; we punish ourselves 365 days a year, 366 in leap years.

It seems like everyone is having more fun than we are. At Indian weddings they paint the bride's hands with henna, there's marigolds everywhere, colorful saris, great food. For us, again it's the chopped liver. And at weddings, *we* step on a glass after we drink wine from it, to remind us that there is always bitter mixed with sweet. A person could get hurt!

We're always kvetching and comparing our troubles. "You think you've got *tsurris*? (That's Yiddish for troubles.) From my *tsurris* you shouldn't know!" It's a contest to see who leads the most miserable existence. Isn't it time to start lightening up a little?

I was recently reading a great book called *Judaikitsch*, which bemoans the lack of kitschy Jewish culture. It shows you how to make a Carmen Miranda yarmulke, a Jewish Princess tiara replete with mini Tab cans and Princess phones, a beaded purse made out of a matzoh farfel box. And it gave me the instructions for making my own Patron

Jew votive candles. This will be a relief to my Jewish friends who have been truly disturbed by all the candles I had in honor of the Virgins of Guadalupe and Santa Maria, of Saint Joseph, of Saint Francis. Hey, I liked the colors.

So here are the ones that are going to grace my house from now on.

"Dr." Estelle, Patron Jew of Love Object Deprivation Disorder, Intercessor for Neurotics. Quote: "There are worse things than no sex. Go read a book."

Ellen, Patron Jew of Medical Bullshit Detection, Intercessor for Jewish Hypochondriacs. Quote: "Your doctor! What does he know?"

Alice, Patron Jew of Plant Rescue, Intercessor for the Horticulturally Challenged. Quote: "Don't throw that out! It's a living thing!"

Elizabeth, Patron Jew of Entertaining, Intercessor of Hostesses. Quote: "You want I should make a tableaux for your centerpiece?"

Aunt Pearl, Patron Jew of Passive Aggressive Compliments, Intercessor for Hostile Relatives. Quote: "That color looks great on you. Maybe *now* someone will ask you out."

Mom, Patron Jew of Guilt, Intercessor for Those Whose Children Never Call. Quote: "I didn't hear from you, I thought you were dead."

And in honor of my favorite dog: Louis, Patron Jew of Schnurring (that's mooching to you non-Yiddish speakers), Intercessor for Freeloaders. Quote: "You can never have too much of a good thing."

For my next project, I'll be making the "Get Lit" Manischewitz-bottle candleholder. I'm gonna have kitschy fun if it kills me. And if it doesn't, you can be sure I'll kvetch about it.

How I Found Peace in the Information Age

I admit it: I don't read or watch or listen to the news anymore. I've stopped my subscriptions to the *New York Times* and *Newsweek*, am working on forgetting *NBC News* anchor's Sue Simmons' smirking face on TV, and have taken the news channels off my AM radio memory buttons.

Medical guru Dr. Andrew Weil says it's really bad for your health to watch the news before you go to bed. I think it's bad to watch it anytime. It's either terribly depressing or it's bad infotainment. I'd rather watch a movie or Animal Planet or *Emeril Live*. I'm definitely drifting into the world of fiction, or Reality Lite. It's so much less stressful.

And that's not the only reason I don't like the news. I am really fussy about the proper use of the English language, and it's being mangled lately. People write or say things like ATM machine, HIV virus, PIN number, VIN number, and are completely unaware of the redundancies. People mix up "your" and "you're," "it's" and "its," and it's making me crazy. When Dubya mispronounces nuclear as "new-kya-lur" I go ballistic. And I can barely contain a scream when someone says "asterick." It's asterisk, with an S. I'd rather read a carefully edited novel by, say, Amy Tan, or a humorous travelogue by Bill Bryson or read anything by my favorite poet, Billy Collins. Those are words with thought behind them.

Trust me, I know what's going on in the world. It's kind of hard not to. If our local and dangerous nuclear facility, Indian Point, closes, or if there's a peace agreement in the Middle East, or if a fat substitute is invented that *doesn't* cause anal leakage, someone will be sure to call me.

Just yesterday my friend Ron called and asked, "Did you see the *Times* today? You have to go read the article on all the hate mail NPR's Yiddish Radio Project is getting. And with Le Pen's election win, it's getting really scary in Europe." With personalized news service like this, I was just a couple of clicks away from reading precisely what I needed to know—online.

I get forwarded emails with great advice on how to repel ticks naturally (a few drops of rose geranium oil on your pet's collar, or on yourself); brilliant articles like the one by Oriana Fallaci, translated from *Corriere della Sera*, on the rise of anti-Semitism in Europe; and news from the front of wherever my friends are around the world. I most certainly do not live with my head in the sand. I e-subscribe to a "take action" website and am alerted when there is a need to write my government representatives about such issues as gay adoption rights in Florida, gun control, and fighting terrorism. (I'm sure there are similar sites for those whose gurus are Patrick Buchanan or Cardinal Egan, so that my paltry little liberal votes are probably cancelled out.)

To those of you who read the newspapers beginning to end, day by day, and leave CNN or BBC America on in the background, I'm grateful to you. Being a news junkie is a nasty job, but someone's gotta do it and I'm just glad it's not me. Thanks to you, I'm sleeping better at night.

Star-Crossed Driver

I read my horoscope one morning, even though I am not sure I really believe that stuff, and I learned that it was a day that Pisces should not venture out.

"Bullshit" I said, and went about my business anyway.

At dinnertime, I decided to go meet a friend for a margarita and a good bowl of guacamole with chips, food of the gods if you ask me. Forget manna and ambrosia, I say margaritas with "guac" and chips (but the guac needs to be made with only avocado, onion, fresh chopped cilantro, minced jalapeños and salt, maybe some diced tomato—nothing more or it's not authentic).

By 10:30, after an uneventful day, I began my drive home, practically cackling that I'd beaten the stars. Then I heard "KACHUNK!" and my tire began to make that "thwacketa-thwacketa" noise that all flats make. "Shit!" I cursed, and drove my limping car into a gas station.

The man behind the counter could not fix flats. He did not even understand me, I don't think, although he did understand some kid who came in and asked for E-Z Widers. Ah, America, land of opportunity, I groused, where people who don't speak English can get jobs in retail. I returned to my car to call my free roadside service dudes who would come and put my spare on. They said no problem, they'd be there in 50 minutes.

I locked my doors and waited. A van pulled up, and three guys got out. One of the guys looked really scary to me. He was tall, dark, had wild black hair, and was wearing a black leather glove on his right hand. I slid lower in my seat, feeling ashamed that I was profiling, something I never did before 9-11. But it wasn't his look that scared me so much as the fact that he was outside the mini-mart punching the air repeatedly with what looked like lethal right hooks.

His companions came out with chips and drinks, and they stood on the curb staring at me. I slid lower still. I pretended to talk on my cell phone. Finally they got in their van and drove away. I exhaled, realizing that I'd been holding my breath.

Then, the van reappeared. Now I was really on the phone. I called the only man I knew I could wake up at 11PM and who I didn't care if he got mad at me, my ex-husband. I told him where I was and what was going on.

"Wanna come keep me company I asked? Or change my tire?"

"No," he said.

"Well I'm scared, and…oh, wait….they're coming toward my car…"

"Who ARE these guys?" he shouted.

"How do I know? Just a minute…" I roll down the window.

Crazy wild man leans in and says in an accent redolent of steel drums, "Miss, would you like us to change your tire for you?"

"Uh, they want to change my tire," I tell the ex. "I'll call you back." I hear him shouting still as I hang up.

Archie, his name turns out to be, is from Trinidad and he has his own waterproofing business out in Queens, New York—you know, the place "The Nanny," played by Fran Drescher, was from. His associate, the one eating the chips, is an ex-cop from NYC. And a third guy, younger, gets to work changing my tire in a flash.

Archie tell me he does a lot of work up here, has even worked locally, in "Cheapaqua."

"Chappaqua," I correct him, wondering if doing so is such a good idea and stifling a giggle at his mispronunciation of the town Bill and Hillary Clinton now call home.

"Yah, Chappaqua," he says, and names all the other towns they work in, "and I've fixed over twenty-five thousand leaky basements."

He hands me a sheaf of flyers, asks me to hand them out for him. I tell him I'll go one better, and write about him.

The tire is changed, the ex-cop tells me to go under 50 driving home, and get right to a tire place in the morning. All three men wish me safe home, as did the ex who I called to inform I was on my way back to my house.

So this little Pisces went "wocketa wocketa" all the way home on her rolling donut, and has learned maybe to trust the stars more. But I've also learned that America still really is the land of opportunity, and I'm grateful to the true kindness of all the Archies who have come here with nothing but dreams and good intentions.

Yes, I Have no Bananas

I love bananas. I especially love them when they have a slight green tinge, and are not sickeningly sweet. I like them raw, and I like them frozen, dipped in chocolate, but only from Dad's in Balboa Island, California. And I love bananas Foster, a dessert dish so decadent I will only eat it if I am out and it's on the menu.

Banana Froz-Fruits, banana chips, Chunky Monkey ice cream—yum. In fruit salads, I'm the one that picks out the banana slices before others can eat them. I even like banana liqueur, but haven't seen any since I was 12, when I sneaked it from my Dad's liquor cabinet in the Canary Islands (they grow bananas there, and there's no drinking age—still, my father was not exactly pleased).

I love bananas so much I once ordered a box of gourmet bananas from a banana farm in California (they're now out of business—I think I was their only customer). There were apple-flavored bananas with a slight crunch to them (this is not as disgusting as it sounds), fat red bananas that tasted faintly pineapple-y, baby bananas, orange bananas, lots of bananas sitting on straw with fancy labels on them and a fancy price tag.

They were delicious, but like all bananas, had to be eaten fast because of the rot factor. I don't like being rushed to eat my food, something my parents could have told you. As a child, many a meal went by with me staring at my food, until, in exasperation, it was taken away from me (or once, dumped on my head). Today, I eat when I want to, and no damn banana is gonna tell me when it's time for chow.

Although I am a gourmet cook, and have not earned the moniker "Condiment Queen" for nothing, a liver-spotted banana does not inspire me to culinary abandon. What can you do with a rotting banana but make banana bread? Let's face it, banana bread is no delicacy, and it's work. Do I need more kitchen work? I think not.

Every time I used to go to the grocery store, I'd buy three bananas. And within days, I considered them to be inedible. I tried refrigerating them to see if it would retard the ripening and sugar production. Aside from turning the skins an alarming, necrotic black, the fridge does nothing to keep them this side of overripe. I've tried slicing and freezing, but frozen bananas on your cornflakes are a true culinary offense. Brain freeze in the morning is too much of a shock for anyone's system.

So, I've stopped buying bananas. Now I play banana roulette. I wait until I'm visiting friends and hope that there are some just-bought bananas, ones that my friends think aren't ripe yet, and ask if I may have one. I bet they are all wondering why I don't buy my own. Sometimes I go weeks with no bananas. Heaven knows if my potassium levels are okay. But now you all know why yes, I have no bananas.

I don't have any milk either, for the same reason. It keeps going bad. I've discovered that half n' half has a much, much, much longer shelf life. And for cereal and cooking? Experiments are currently underway in the Appleton household comparing soy milk, rice milk and almond milk. Stay tuned for the results. But if you visit, don't expect any bananas on your cereal.

Mailbox Macho

When I was little, nobody had mailboxes. We had those little slots in the front door and the postman (it was always a man then) walked up and pushed the mail through. Lucky—Harry and Bea Smollene's dog—who lived next door to us, used to go crazy when the letters came fluttering through the door, and Bea thought that was just a fine way for Lucky to get her exercise.

In Europe, where I lived for several years, we used to pick up our mail at the post office, and it was a very social event. Everyone was in everyone else's business, and if you were a foreigner you inspired a great deal of curiosity. There was lots of gossip about us, which the Europeans thought I couldn't understand, but one of my main survival defenses as a child was to learn the language of every country we lived in. So I was able to report to my father that not only had his Motion Picture Welfare check arrived but also the exact amount that I overheard the postmistress (because it was always a woman then) tell everyone, even before he opened it. I never got why he was so annoyed.

I thought getting your mail at the post office was just a European thing until I moved to Goldens Bridge, then a little town an hour or so north of New York City, in the days when we still dialed only 4 digits to reach each other by phone. There, we'd stand in line and listen to who'd had a baby and was it born vaginally or by C-section and how long the labor took, or other intimate details of the lives of locals. It took freakin' forever to pick up the mail.

So the day we got home delivery was really exciting. We actually had a formal meeting with our neighbors to decide what kind of mailboxes to buy, since we were going to go "high tech" and put four boxes on one stand. We delegated who'd build, who'd design, what kind of numbers to put on, who'd buy what and where the best places were to purchase. Let's face it, we were such novices, you'd think we'd never had received a letter before in our lives.

The mailman (and it was a guy) wasn't quite sure how the new system worked, either. He'd leave the flag up when our mail had been delivered, and finally my pre-pubescent son wrote a note explaining to the mailman that it was US who put the flag up to tell him if we had mail for HIM to pick up. But he never got it, so we learned to live in mailbox flag confusion.

Then I left Goldens Bridge and moved to the land of McMansions and fancy mailboxes. Most of them were kind of cute, if a little cheesy. Painted vines, special vinyl covers from the bird store depicting cardinals or bluejays, nice classy lettering and numbers. There were also the "I-dare-you-to-knock-me-down-with-a-baseball-bat-when-you-are-out-driving-drunk-with-your-fuckwit-buddies" mailboxes, big ol' plastic things sunk in the ground into cement pilings. Ugly.

But I had not seen ugly until the latest McMansions went up around the corner from me, and one of the owners put up his ode-to-the-country mailbox, a huge wooden rooster with a crown of black painted feathers. It is so obscene that I want to become a mailbox anarchist and do things to it, like put little bonnets on, or sprigs of plastic fruit *a la* Carmen Miranda. But I won't because now they'd know it was me.

The only satisfaction I get from this hideous thing is that it's a good landmark. I can tell people, when I am giving directions to my house, "Turn right after the big cock." Which, believe you me, feels really good to say.

The Big Five-Oh

On February 29th 2002, I turn fifty. Okay, so it's on March 1st this year—I get a one-day reprieve. I can pretend all I want that I am really twelve, but fact is, while I have only had twelve birthdays, I've been alive 50 years. The thought of being this age terrifies me, because that's the age my mother was when she dropped dead.

Now, I am nothing like my mother, except in build. I never gave my children coffee enemas, or made them eat only fertilized eggs and drink only juices squeezed from a noisy extractor. I never went to a psychic instead of a doctor. I did not force my kids to go to a Waldorf School. I don't play bridge. And I do not smoke two packs of cigarettes a day.

Although I was never a good enough hippie, I think I've been a credit to my fellow boomers. I've burned bras, eschewed shaving (legs and armpits), had my consciousness raised, practiced meditation, marched for peace and justice and freedom of choice, given birth out-of-hospital, nursed my babies, worn natural fibers, and been a devoted recycler. I've refrained from eating non-union grapes, eating at Denny's or Cracker Barrel (racist and homophobic, respectively), and eating the brown acid. Or any acid.

There's plenty in my life I haven't done, and have no desire to. Take bungee jumping. Skydiving. Shooting someone. Shooting smack. But I have shot the moon playing Hearts, which, if you have, you know is enough to make anyone feel pretty smug.

I've also been a rape counselor, an abortion counselor, a childbirth educator. I've attended untold births and witnessed the miracle of life over and over. I can cook practically anything. I can paint. I can write. I can tickle. I can kiss. I have lived, laughed, loved, and lost. And I really do dance like no one is watching.

Now here I am, about to cross over. Either into my next 50 years, or into the spirit world. I haven't inhaled anything since my college days, I exercise regularly enough, my weight's okay, my blood pressure and cholesterol are down, and my hot flashes are manageable (and thank you for asking). I've been so good you could puke. Still, I'm scared. Genes is genes.

So if I make it to fifty years and three months, and don't share my mother's tragic fate, there will be joy throughout the land. I am going to throw all caution away. I'll start eating Cheetos and wearing skimpy polyester thongs. I'll go to bed when I want and wake up when I want. I'll hang out in smoky bars and have more than one drink. I'm gonna live like crazy. And you'll know it, too, because that will be me you see on the back of someone's Harley, red streaks in my hair, not wearing a helmet or sunscreen, swigging from an open bottle of scotch, smoking a Phillies Blunt, and having unsafe sex—all at the same time. I am not going gently into that next half-century.

0-595-26528-6